Coconut Milk Ice Cream

Copyright © 2014, Aimee Ryan
Self published
www.wallflowergirl.co.uk

All rights reserved. No part of this book may be reproduced without the Author's permission. Brief excerpts may be used for the purpose of a review only.

Coconut Milk Ice Cream

Ice creams & other frozen treats
made from coconut milk

80+ Vegan &
Grain-free recipes

Written and photographed by
Aimee Ryan

CONTENTS

Introduction..6
Why Coconut Milk?...7
Health Benefits...8
Ingredients..10
Special Diets & Substitutions...................................16
Tools & Equipment..18
Making The Perfect Ice Cream.................................20
Recipes
    Ice Creams 23
    Frozen Desserts & Treats................................111
    Cones, Toppings & Sauces..............................136
Resources...154
Index...156

INTRODUCTION

This is a book dedicated to my love of coconut milk ice cream.

Despite not being a vegan myself, I love experimenting with diet and allergy- friendly recipes. After discovering the use of coconut milk in ice creams, I've not looked back. I love the taste, the texture and the healthiness is a bonus!

I was very pleasantly surprised at how adaptable coconut milk ice creams could be and how well the coconut milk works with other flavours, regardless of whether they usually go well with coconut or not. You can enhance the coconut taste if you want, pairing it with extra coconut and tropical flavours. Or you can simply use it as an ice cream base and add any flavour from coffee to lavender, without it clashing. It never overpowers the ice cream.

I've been experimenting with coconut milk ice creams for a couple of years now and have learned a lot through trial and error. I know the effects of using or leaving out certain ingredients can have on the end result and have now "perfected" the coconut milk ice cream formula!

If you're vegan, lactose intolerant, if you have an egg allergy or just want to eat healthier, these ice creams are for you. I'll show you the best ingredients, methods and tools to use to create the perfect vegan ice creams at home. I hope you enjoy!

Aimee

WHY COCONUT MILK?

Because it makes the best ice cream! It's high fat content improves the texture and taste by making a super creamy ice cream. Not only does it rival ordinary ice cream in texture and taste, but it's a lot healthier for you too. I discuss some of the health benefits on the next page but have also included healthy sweeteners and add-ins to make these recipes extra healthy without compromising on taste.

Can you taste the coconut in these ice creams?

No, not all of them. Some recipes enhance the coconut flavour and some completely mask it. The coconut milk acts as the ice cream base and isn't an overpowering flavour at all. Even non-coconut fans will enjoy these ice creams!

Is it easy to get hold of?

Very! Almost all supermarkets, Asian food markets and health food shops supply coconut milk. You can also make your own at home (see page 13.)

Is it expensive to make?

When you compare the cost of the cream, milk and eggs you'd need in ordinary ice cream recipes, coconut milk ice creams shouldn't cost you any extra and perhaps even less, assuming you aren't using especially expensive add-ins.

Can I use other types of milk substitutes for these recipes?

The short answer is no. The creaminess and fat content of the coconut milk is what makes these ice creams work so well. Simply swapping them for another type of milk will result in a watery, ice and hard ice cream. You would need to supplement it with some type of cream.

HEALTH BENEFITS

I don't want to get too bogged down about nutrition in this book. I use coconut in my ice creams, simply because I love the creamy texture and taste, without the need for dairy or eggs. But coconuts do offer plenty of health benefits that are worth sharing...

Weight management

The medium-chain fats found in coconut are used immediately by the body as a source of energy which increases metabolism and prevents excess fat storage. It also helps reduce sweet cravings, leaves you feeling fuller for longer and balances insulin levels.

Digestion

Coconuts are very high in fibre, helping digestive problems and regulating bowel movements. It has been said that it also helps the body's ability to absorb certain minerals.

Immune boosting

Coconuts have antibacterial, anti-fungal, anti-viral and anti-parasitic properties that help strengthen the immune system and lower incidences of sickness.

Skin & hair

Coconuts are renowned for their skin and hair benefits. Coconut *oil* can double as a natural sunscreen, moisturiser, conditioner and even a make-up remover! It also helps with skin conditions such as eczema and acne.

Heart health

The fats in coconut contain no cholesterol and even helps improve your cholesterol profile.

& lot's more!

What about saturated fats?

Coconuts are high in saturated fats but this isn't always bad news, contrary to what we've been led to believe. There are different lengths of saturated fat chains and these impact the body in different ways...

The Long Chain Triglycerides (LCT) found primarily in animal products, are very difficult for the body to breakdown and leads to excess fat storage. But the Medium Chain Triglycerides (MCT) found in coconuts, are immediately metabolised by the body. The metabolic process actually uses up more calories than the fat contains.

So don't be scared of the fats in coconut, it's good for you and will even help you lose weight, if that's your goal. Ice cream all round!

INGREDIENTS

An A-Z on some of the main ingredients used in my recipes. I've tried to avoid expensive and hard-to-get-hold-of ingredients but if you're struggling to get find anything, please see my resources list on page 154.

Alcohol
As alcohol does not freeze, using a little bit of it helps keep the ice creams from freezing too hard. It is also used for flavour in some of the recipes. Choose an inexpensive but good tasting liquor.

If you're going to be serving the ice cream to kids or someone avoiding alcohol, it should be omitted from the recipe.

Almond flour / ground Almonds
Ground almonds are made from blanched almonds - which means the skin has been removed. Almond flour can be used but almond meal is different and won't give the same results as it's coarser and contains the skin of the almonds.

It's great to bake with, low in carbs and high in protein! Ground almonds are very easy to come by in UK supermarkets and almond flour can be purchased in most health food stores in the US.

Almond milk
Almond milk is a common alternative to dairy milk and is rich in nutrients. It's lighter than coconut milk and I tend to use it when I'm looking for a thinner or more pourable texture, such as in my milkshake recipes. It can be found in some supermarkets and most health food shops.

Arrowroot powder
Arrowroot is a grain-free starch, similar to cornstarch and is commonly used for thickening sauces. It's used in these ice creams to help thicken the mixture and create a custard-like base. It needs to be heated at a high temperature to activate it's thickening properties and is usually done so by mixing into a slurry or paste and adding to the boiling ice cream mixture. It can be found at most supermarkets and health food stores.

Chocolate
Choose a dark chocolate with a minimum of 70% solids. Most dark chocolate is dairy-free and vegan-friendly but always check the ingredients. Some bars and bags of chips are made in factories that contain dairy and gluten. If you need help finding dairy-free / vegan-friendly chocolate, see my resources list on page 154.

Cocoa powder
Make sure you use an unsweetened cocoa powder with no added ingredients. Raw cocoa powder is best.

Coconut flakes & desiccated coconut
Coconut flakes are generally large, unsweetened flakes of coconut, whereas desiccated coconut is finer and *usually* sweetened. I use unsweetened coconut flakes to make homemade coconut milk and they also makes a great ice cream topping. They can be found at most supermarkets and health food shops.

Coconut flour
I love using coconut flour in gluten-free baking but the only downside is that it usually requires a lot of eggs, so I've used mainly almond flour instead. It also makes a good binder and thickener. Coconut flour can be found in most health food stores or online.

Coconut milk
The star ingredient! Coconut milk is the base ingredient in most of these recipes. When buying, make sure you choose a ***full-fat*** variety. Full fat milk will separate (the cream will float to the top) so for accurate measuring, you may need to whisk the milk on a low heat to make it all the same consistency first. Coconut milk can be bought in supermarkets, Asian food shops and health food shops. Even better, learn how to make your own on page 13, where you can also learn how to make evaporated coconut milk, condensed coconut milk and coconut cream.

Coconut oil
Always choose an unrefined virgin coconut oil, packaged in a clear glass jar. It makes an excellent oil for frying and adds a subtle but not too overpowering coconut taste to dishes. I tend to use it in place of butter and to thin-out some of the sauces. It's a popular health food found in most health food stores and online.

Coconut sugar
Coconut sugar is derived from coconut sap. I love the taste of this sugar, it's similar to brown sugar but with a delicious caramel taste. It's not to be confused with palm sugar which has a completely different taste. Coconut sugar is low GI, very rich in minerals and can be used 1:1 in place of regular sugar. It can be found at most health food stores or online. See my resources list on page 154 for suggestions.

Coffee
I've used instant coffee in these recipes but try and use a strong, good quality brand to give a nicer flavour.

Fruits
All fruits and berries used are fresh, unless otherwise stated. Frozen berries work quite well in these recipes but make sure they are defrosted before using.
Dried fruit, such as dates and raisins are used to add extra sweetness and texture to some recipes. Make sure you buy organic with no added sweeteners or preservatives.

Maple syrup
Maple syrup is my main sweetener of choice. It's vegan, rich in minerals and antioxidants and gives a gorgeous, rich flavour. It can be found in most supermarkets and health food stores but use a good quality one. If you prefer, agave nectar can be used instead, using equal amounts.

Nuts & nut butters
All nuts used are raw and whole, unless otherwise stated. The nut butters, however, are usually made from roasted nuts - this is for improved flavour. If you prefer, you can use raw nut butters but please note that the taste will be different. Peanut butter is easy to find in most shops but other nut butters such as almond, hazelnut and cashew, can be found in health food stores or online.

Vanilla paste & extract
When it comes to making vanilla ice cream, I prefer to use vanilla paste or the contents of a vanilla pod. This gives a more intense flavour and those little black specks you expect to see in a good quality vanilla ice cream. I use vanilla extract in other recipes where I just want a small hint of vanilla. Both the paste and extracts can be found in most supermarkets or specialist baking shops.

Xylitol
When it comes to sugar-free recipes, Xylitol is my sweetener of choice. Firstly, the taste is far better than other sugar-free sweeteners I've tried and doesn't leave you with a yucky after-taste. Secondly, it's much easier to get hold of and cheaper to buy. It can be used 1:1 with ordinary sugar. A lot of supermarkets in the UK sell Xylitol but you can also find it in health food shops and online.

Important: Xylitol is toxic to dogs, so if you own one, make sure you keep the Xylitol out of reach.

HOMEMADE COCONUT MILK

Yields approx 840ml / 3 ½ cups

Making your own coconut milk at home is a lot easier than you might think and it's better for you too. Homemade coconut milk will separate (the fat will rise to the top) so when you're measuring it out for recipes, you may need to whisk it over a low heat first to make it all the same consistency again.

You will need:
200g / 2 cups shredded coconut flakes (unsweetened) or fresh grated coconut
3 cups of hot water
A blender
A colander
2 layers of cheesecloth

Tip the shredded coconut into a blender and pour over the hot water. Blend for about 3 minutes until thick and creamy.

Prepare a large saucepan or bowl and place the colander on top. Lay the cheesecloth over the colander and pour the mixture onto it. Gather the edges of the cloth and twist together. Squeeze as much of the liquid into the bowl as you can.

The leftover coconut fibre can be used to make coconut flour! See the next page on how to do this, where you will also see how to make coconut cream, evaporated milk and condensed milk. Store the milk in an airtight jar in the fridge for up to 5 days.

COCONUT MILK ICE CREAM

How to make...

Evaporated coconut milk
Pour 480ml / 2 cups of coconut milk into a saucepan and let it simmer slowly on very low heat until reduced. After approximately 20 – 30 minutes you will have 360ml / 1 - 1 ½ cups of evaporated milk.

Condensed coconut milk
Pour 480ml / 2 cups of coconut milk into a saucepan and whisk on medium heat. After about 5 minutes when it begins to boil, reduce the heat to a simmer and whisk in 60ml / ¼ cup maple syrup. Leave to simmer for another 30 minutes until the milk has reduced to about 360ml / 1 - 1 ½ cups of condensed milk.

Coconut cream
Coconut cream is the thick substance that floats to the top of the coconut milk. If you have a can of coconut milk, you can just spoon the cream off the top. Make sure you use a full fat can without emulsifiers (which makes the coconut milk the same consistency throughout.) Homemade coconut milk should separate from the watery liquid when chilled, leaving you the cream at the top.

Use it to make a delicious whipped cream! (See page 148.)

Coconut flour
After making homemade coconut milk, spread the leftover coconut pulp onto a baking sheet lined with parchment paper. Either dry in the oven at a low temperature (120°C / 230°F) for 45 minutes - 1 hour or use a dehydrator to dry the pulp out until all the moisture has evaporated, leaving you with a coarse flour.

Tip the dried pulp into a food processor or high-powered blender and mix until you have a fine flour. Store in an air-tight container and use for baking!

SPECIAL DIETS & SUBSTITUTIONS

All ingredients used in this book are vegan, dairy-free, gluten-free and grain-free.

Vegan, egg-free & dairy-free
All these recipes are free from eggs, dairy and other animal products and are all made to be specifically vegan-friendly. But when a recipe calls for dark chocolate, make sure you are using a vegan-approved or dairy-free chocolate. Most dark chocolate is, but it's best to check! See my resources list on page 154.

Gluten-free
Whether you're a celiac, gluten-intolerant or following a grain-free diet, all these recipes are free from gluten and grains! Make sure you use a gluten-free dark chocolate, when called for.

Raw
If you're on a raw diet, you can easily make a lot of the ice creams in this book with a few tweaks...

Leave out any cooking, arrowroot powder and alcohol.* Use a raw coconut milk (preferably homemade, see page 13) a raw friendly sweetener such as agave syrup, use a raw vanilla powder or vanilla pods and use raw chocolate in place of dark, if needed.

*Please note that when you leave out the arrowroot powder and alcohol, this will make the ice cream harder and less creamy - to counteract this, I suggest using coconut cream (see page 14) in place of coconut milk.

Sugar-free

The recipes in this book contain no refined sugars and use mainly maple syrup and coconut sugar. However, if you're avoiding or trying to cut down on sugar altogether, or if you're diabetic or if you're on a low carb diet - it's easy to make most of these ice creams sugar-free, as well as most of the sauces, cones and toppings.

As a general rule, you can substitute ½ cup maple syrup for ¾ cup xylitol or 1 cup erythritol.

If you're avoiding starch, leave out the arrowroot powder. See notes above on leaving this out.

Please note: These substitutions are just guidelines and have not necessarily been tested out on these recipes.

Soy-free

All these ice creams and recipes are free from soy, that is assuming you use a soy-free chocolate, when called for. See my resources list on page 154 for recommendations.

TOOLS & EQUIPMENT

A guide to the essential tools & equipment you'll need to make the best ice cream at home.

Ice cream makers

This is the main piece of equipment you'll need to make ice creams and you really don't need to spend a lot of money on a state-of-the-art one to make decent ice creams. I spent less than £30 on mine! The more affordable ones tend to be the machines where you need to pre-freeze the bowl before churning, usually for 24 hours. My ice cream maker is quite small so I keep the bowl in the freezer all the time for convenience.

All ice cream makers vary, so make sure you read the instruction manual and follow the guidelines. Most manufacturers suggest churning for 20 minutes but it could be a little more or less.

The recipes in this book all make up approximately 2 pints / 1 quart of ice cream, which tends to be the minimum ice cream makers hold but you can simply halve or even double the recipe depending on your needs.

On page 22 I will show you how you can make ice creams without an ice cream maker, although, I really do recommend buying one if you plan on making them often and want the best result.

Baking sheets & roasting dishes
You'll need these for roasting fruits & nuts, making granitas and baking the brownies and cookies for ice cream sandwiches.

Blenders & food processors
A blender is essential for creating smooth mixtures. You can use a stand blender, wand blender or a food processor with sharp blades. I usually use my food processor for chopping and grinding nuts but you can also chop the nuts with a knife or use a food mill to grind them.

Containers
You will need freezer-safe containers for storing your homemade ice creams. These recipes yield approximately 2 pints / 1 quart of ice cream so make sure you find a suitable sized container. I like using square pyrex containers with lids but a sturdy plastic container will work well.

Grater & zester
Hand-held zesters are recommended for zesting citrus fruits. They're easier to use and remove the zest without taking too much pith with it.

Ice cream scoops
My favourite ice cream scoop to use is the trigger or spring-loaded type which always gives the perfect, clean, rounded scoop. It uses a small metal strip inside the scoop to create the rounded shape. I also have a traditional solid ice cream scoop which is good for using on extra firm ice creams. Most ice cream scoops are not dishwasher friendly so always wash by hand.

Measuring cups & scales
I mostly measure in grams because I find it the most accurate. I do find cup measurements handy sometimes though, especially for liquids and have included both types of measurements in this book. I've also added a grams to ounces conversion table at the back of the book. (See page 155.)

Mixing bowls
I find small bowls very useful for mixing pastes and measuring out ingredients. I tend to mix the ice creams in a saucepan but like to transfer the ice cream mixtures to a heat-proof bowl to store in the fridge until it cools.

Parchment paper
Parchment paper is a non-stick, oven-safe paper that is used to line baking trays and wrap foods. Do not use greaseproof paper as it is not as effective and can burn in the oven.

Saucepans
You will need a saucepan large enough to hold the volume of ice cream mixture, allowing room for whisking and thickening. I also use a small saucepan for making sauces and coulis.

Sieves
A fine mesh sieve is required for straining out ingredients used for flavourings.

Waffle cone maker
If you want to make professional-looking ice cream cones at home on a regular basis, you might want to get a waffle cone maker but they definitely are a luxury item and aren't strictly necessary! Although, the basic machines don't tend to be very expensive.

For making ice cream cones, there is one thing you will need - a cone shaper. This is an object with a handle that you use to roll the waffle into a cone.

Whisks
Hand held whisks are recommended but electric whisks are handy for some recipes such as whipped cream and the baking recipes.

MAKING THE PERFECT ICE CREAM

One of the benefits of coconut milk ice cream is that it's easier and quicker to make than ordinary ice creams. That being said, there are still some tricks and tips I recommend you follow to get the absolute best results.

Making a custard-like base using arrowroot powder

Most traditional ice cream recipes start with a thick, creamy custard base made using cream, milk, sugar and eggs. We want to create a base with similar properties but without the need for those ingredients. To do this, we use arrowroot powder.

If you've used arrowroot before to thicken a sauce, you will understand why it works so well in these ice creams. When mixed with a liquid and exposed to a high heat, it creates a thick, custard-like consistency.

So to make a basic ice cream base you need 720ml / 3 cups of coconut milk (which substitutes the cream and milk); 120ml / ½ cup of maple syrup (the main choice of sweetener in these recipes); 2 tbsp arrowroot powder (which replaces the need for eggs).
Start by mixing a small amount (about 60ml / ¼ cup) of the coconut milk, cold or room temperature, with the arrowroot powder in a small bowl. Whisk until it's dissolved in the water. I like to use a small whisk or a fork to do this.

Then pour the rest of the coconut milk into a large saucepan with the maple syrup, stirring to combine the two. As mentioned, the arrowroot needs to be exposed to a high heat to activate it's thickening properties, so heat the saucepan on a medium heat and bring to a boil. When it begins to boil, it's time to add the arrowroot mixture. Spoon the mixture into the saucepan, lower the heat and whisk for a few seconds until you notice the mixture thickening. At this point you'll want to remove the pan from the heat.

Mix-ins

Once the ice cream base has been made, I like to stir in 1 tbsp of alcohol. Alcohol does not freeze so adding it to the mixture helps the ice cream stay a little softer and scoop-able. This is also the time to add in any flavour extracts such as vanilla extract.

Chilling your ice cream mixture

It's very important to let your ice cream mixture become completely cold before trying to churn it. I recommend leaving it overnight in the fridge and perhaps in the freezer for 10 minutes before churning.

When the ice cream mixture chills, it may form a very slight "skin" or become lumpy, because of the arrowroot. This is nothing to worry about and will disappear during churning.

Churning

Just as you want to make sure your ice cream mixture is completely cold, you want to make sure the ice cream maker bowl is completely frozen. It's best to leave it in the freezer for at least 24 hours. It's not always convenient to wait this long - during the making of this book I had to buy an extra bowl to allow me to make more ice creams without having to wait for the other bowl to freeze.

Pour or spoon the mixture into your ice cream maker and follow the manufacturer's instructions. It usually takes about 20-25 minutes for the ice cream to churn but you'll know when it's ready by looking at the mixture. It will be thick, look like soft ice cream and the paddle will slow down. When it's ready, turn off the machine and spoon the mixture into a freezer-safe container. A large, shallow container is best for keeping a creamy consistency.

Churning without an ice cream machine

As I mentioned before, I strongly recommend buying an ice cream machine - even if it's just a cheap one but if you'd like to try churning without, here is the best way...

The main benefit of using an ice cream machine is the amount of air it gets into the mixture so we need to make sure we do the same here. Firstly, make sure your mixture is chilled and transfer to a freezer-safe container and place in the freezer. Leave it for 30 minutes.

After 30 minutes, take the container out and give it a good whisk with an electric hand-held mixer. This will break up any ice that has begun to form and incorporate some air into it. After it's been thoroughly mixed, return it to the freezer straight away. Freeze for another 30 minutes and repeat the whisking process. Keep alternating the whisking and freezing every 30 minutes, for about 3 hours, until it's frozen.

Storing

Most ice creams can be stored in the freezer for about three months. If you're making a few different flavours, I recommend labelling the containers for convenience.

Serving

Homemade ice creams almost always have a harder consistency than store-bought. This is because there are no stabilizers or other unpronounceable ingredients that cause the ice cream to stay soft. So when you want to serve the ice cream, leave the container out at room temperature for about 10 minutes (or in the fridge for approximately 15 minutes) before scooping. When it's softened slightly but is still nice and firm, scoop it into a bowl or ice cream dish.

To get the perfect, cleanest look, I like to dip the ice cream scoop in hot water for a few seconds before and in-between scoops. Serve immediately.

Return any unused ice cream straight back into the freezer, as soon as possible. Do not attempt to re-freeze melted ice cream as it will freeze into a solid block.

There are plenty of recipes for sauces, toppings and even vegan & grain-free cones in this book, so why not dress your ice cream up a bit!

ICE CREAMS

HEALTHY SPINS ON FAMOUS FLAVOURS

Vanilla..26
Chocolate...27
Cashew Cookie Dough Chip...................28
Chocolate Chip......................................30
Chocolate Brownie.................................31
Salted Caramel......................................32
Mint Chocolate Chip..............................34
Mocha...35

 Vanilla

Yields approx 2 pints / 1 quart

I know some people will probably find me boring for this, but vanilla is still one of my most favourite flavours. Sometimes you just can't beat it. I like to use vanilla paste or the contents of a vanilla pod to get a more "real" flavour and those little black dots that let you know you're eating a good quality vanilla ice cream.

720ml / 3 cups coconut milk
2 tbsp arrowroot powder
120ml / ½ cup maple syrup
2 tbsp vanilla paste
(optional) 1 tbsp alcohol

Mix 60ml / ¼ cup coconut milk with the arrowroot powder in a small bowl and set aside.

Pour the rest of the coconut milk and the maple syrup into a large saucepan and bring to a boil. As soon as the mixture begins to boil, stir in the arrowroot mixture to thicken the liquid. Remove from the heat and stir in the vanilla and alcohol.

Chill the mixture in the fridge until cold and churn.

Transfer the ice cream to a freezer-safe container and freeze for at least 3 hours or overnight.

Chocolate

Yields approx 2 pints / 1 quart

Rich, dark chocolate ice cream. If you're a chocolate-lover, you can't go wrong with this one.

720ml / 3 cups coconut milk
2 tbsp arrowroot powder
20g / ¼ cup cocoa powder
120ml / ½ cup maple syrup
1 tsp vanilla extract
90g / ½ cup dark chocolate chips
(optional) 1 tbsp alcohol

Mix 60ml / ¼ cup coconut milk with the arrowroot powder in a small bowl and set aside.

Pour the rest of the coconut milk, the cocoa powder and maple syrup into a large saucepan and bring to a boil, stirring all the time. As soon as the mixture begins to boil, stir in the arrowroot mixture to thicken the liquid. Remove from the heat and stir in the vanilla, chocolate chips and alcohol. Keep stirring until all the chocolate is melted.

Chill the mixture in the fridge until cold and churn.

Transfer the ice cream to a freezer-safe container and freeze for at least 3 hours or overnight.

Cashew Cookie Dough Chip

Yields approx 2 pints / 1 quart

This cookie dough is so good and you wouldn't know it was healthy too. I like to eat the cookie dough on it's own just as a snack but it's even better in this ice cream. The texture is just like store-bought but with the addition of a subtle cashew taste.

For the raw cookie dough:
2 tbsp cashew butter
1 tbsp coconut flour
1 tbsp maple syrup
1 tsp vanilla extract

For the ice cream:
720ml / 3 cups coconut milk
2 tbsp arrowroot powder
120ml / ½ cup maple syrup
1 tbsp vanilla extract
(optional) 1 tbsp alcohol
90g / ½ cup dark chocolate chips

To make the cookie dough, combine all the ingredients in a food processor until it forms a soft but firm dough. Roll together small pea-sized balls of the dough to form the cookie dough chunks. Refrigerate whilst you make the ice cream.

To make the ice cream, mix 60ml / ¼ cup coconut milk with the arrowroot powder in a small bowl and set aside.

Pour the rest of the coconut milk and maple syrup into a large saucepan and bring to a boil. As soon as the mixture begins to boil, stir in the arrowroot mixture to thicken the liquid. Remove from the heat and stir in the vanilla and alcohol.

Chill the mixture in the fridge until cold and churn. During the last few minutes of churning, add in the cookie dough and chocolate chips.

Transfer the ice cream to a freezer-safe container and freeze for at least 3 hours or overnight.

Chocolate Chip

Yields approx 2 pints / 1 quart

If you can't decide between vanilla and chocolate, this ice cream has the best of both worlds. I love the smooth creaminess of the ice cream with the small chocolatey crunch of the chocolate chips.

720ml / 3 cups coconut milk
2 tbsp arrowroot powder
120ml / ½ cup maple syrup
1 tsp vanilla extract
(optional) 1 tbsp alcohol
135g / ¾ cup dark chocolate chips

Mix 60ml / ¼ cup coconut milk with the arrowroot powder in a small bowl and set aside.

Pour the rest of the coconut milk and the maple syrup into a large saucepan and bring to a boil. As soon as the mixture begins to boil, stir in the arrowroot mixture to thicken the liquid. Remove from the heat and stir in the vanilla and alcohol.

Chill the mixture in the fridge until cold and churn. During the last few minutes of churning, add in the chocolate chips. I like to chop the chocolate chips in the food processor for a few seconds to create a more "speckled" effect in the ice cream.

Transfer the ice cream to a freezer-safe container and freeze for at least 3 hours or overnight.

Chocolate Brownie

Yields approx 2 pints / 1 quart

If chocolate chips don't sound devilish enough for you, try some chocolate brownie pieces instead.

720ml / 3 cups coconut milk
2 tbsp arrowroot powder
120ml / ½ cup maple syrup
1 tsp vanilla extract
(optional) 1 tbsp alcohol

1 cup chocolate brownies broken into small pieces (approx ⅓ of a batch, see page 118)

Variation: Add 2 tbsp cocoa powder to the ice cream mixture to make it extra chocolatey!

Mix 60ml / ¼ cup coconut milk with the arrowroot powder in a small bowl and set aside.

Pour the rest of the coconut milk and the maple syrup into a large saucepan and bring to a boil. As soon as the mixture begins to boil, stir in the arrowroot mixture to thicken the liquid. Remove from the heat and stir in the vanilla and alcohol.

Chill the mixture in the fridge until cold and churn. During the last few minutes of churning, add in the chocolate brownie pieces.

Transfer the ice cream to a freezer-safe container and freeze for at least 3 hours or overnight.

COCONUT MILK ICE CREAM

Salted Caramel

Yields approx 2 pints / 1 quart

One of the simplest ice creams to make, yet perhaps the most impressive flavour. The caramel comes from the coconut sugar which has a naturally strong caramel taste. It makes this ice cream a lot healthier than other salted caramel ice creams but tastes just as amazing!

720ml / 3 cups coconut milk
2 tbsp arrowroot powder
140g / 1 cup coconut sugar*
1 tsp coarse sea salt
2 tsp vanilla extract
(optional) 1 tbsp alcohol

*Make sure you use coconut sugar and not palm sugar

Mix 60ml / ¼ cup coconut milk with the arrowroot powder in a small bowl and set aside.

Pour the rest of the coconut milk into a large saucepan with the coconut sugar and salt. As soon as the mixture begins to boil, stir in the arrowroot mixture to thicken the liquid. Remove from the heat and stir in the vanilla and alcohol.

Chill in the fridge until cold and churn. Transfer the ice cream to a freezer-safe container and freeze for at least 3 hours or overnight.

COCONUT MILK ICE CREAM

Mint Chocolate Chip

Yields approx 2 pints / 1 quart

A secretly healthy Mint Chocolate Chip ice cream with avocado, masked by the strong peppermint flavour. The avocado adds an extra creaminess to this ice cream, furthering the indulgence. I love the colour it gives too - green with speckled chocolate!

720ml / 3 cups coconut milk
2 tbsp arrowroot powder
2 small ripe avocados
120ml / ½ cup maple syrup
1 tsp peppermint extract
(optional) 1 tbsp alcohol
90g / ½ cup dark chocolate chips

Mix 60ml / ¼ cup coconut milk with the arrowroot powder in a small bowl and set aside.

Cut the avocado in half, remove the stone and scoop out the flesh into a blender. Pour the rest of the coconut milk and the maple syrup in with it and mix until completely smooth.

Pour the mixture into a large saucepan and bring to a boil. As soon as the mixture begins to boil, stir in the arrowroot mixture to thicken the liquid. Remove from the heat and stir in the vanilla and alcohol.

Chill the mixture in the fridge until cold and churn. During the last few minutes of churning, add chocolate chips. I like to blitz the chocolate chips in a food processor for a few seconds beforehand to give the ice cream more of a speckled effect.

Transfer the ice cream to a freezer-safe container and freeze for at least 3 hours or overnight

Mocha

Yields approx 2 pints / 1 quart

A strong, energizing coffee & chocolate ice cream, perfect after a meal or when you need a "pick me up!"

720ml / 3 cups coconut milk
2 tbsp arrowroot powder
2 tbsp instant ground coffee
2 tbsp cocoa powder
120ml / ½ cup maple syrup
1 tsp vanilla extract
(optional) 1 tbsp alcohol

Mix 60ml / ¼ cup coconut milk with the arrowroot powder in a small bowl and set aside.

Pour the rest of the coconut milk into a large saucepan with the coffee, cocoa powder and maple syrup and bring to a boil. As soon as the mixture begins to boil, stir in the arrowroot mixture to thicken the liquid. Remove from the heat and stir in the vanilla and alcohol.

Chill the mixture in the fridge until cold and churn.

Transfer the ice cream to a freezer-safe container and freeze for at least 3 hours or overnight.

FRUITY FLAVOURS

Coconut 37
Mango & Passionfruit.......................38
Roasted Pineapple............................40
Papaya & Lime...................................41
Roasted Plum & Cardamom...............42
Pomegranate.....................................44
Sweet Melon......................................45
Date..46
Strawberry...48
Caramelized Banana.........................49
Peaches & Cream..............................50
Orange...52
Apricot...53

Coconut

Yields approx 2 pints / 1 quart

I couldn't write a book about coconut milk ice creams and not include a coconut flavour ice cream! Serve with fresh pineapple and mango chunks for a tropical treat.

720ml / 3 cups coconut milk
2 tbsp arrowroot powder
120ml / ½ cup maple syrup
1 tsp vanilla extract
(optional) 1 tbsp alcohol
80g / ½ cup desiccated coconut

Mix 60ml / ¼ cup coconut milk with the arrowroot powder in a small bowl and set aside.

Pour the rest of the coconut milk into a large saucepan with the maple syrup and bring to a boil. As soon as the mixture begins to boil, stir in the arrowroot mixture to thicken the liquid. Remove from the heat and stir in the vanilla and alcohol.

Chill the mixture in the fridge until cold and churn. During the last few minutes of churning, add in the desiccated coconut.

Transfer the ice cream to a freezer-safe container and freeze for at least 3 hours or overnight.

Mango & Passionfruit

Yields approx 2 pints / 1 quart

Something about the mango adds even more creaminess to this ice cream. The combination of the mango and passionfruit is one of my favourites, it's just so moreish.

720ml / 3 cups coconut milk
2 tbsp arrowroot powder
120ml / ½ cup maple syrup
2 medium-sized mangos, diced
Pulp from 8 passion fruits
1 tsp vanilla extract
(optional) 1 tbsp alcohol

Mix 60ml / ¼ cup coconut milk with the arrowroot powder in a small bowl and set aside.

Pour the rest of the coconut milk into a blender with the maple syrup, mango chunks and passion fruit pulp (reserve some for decoration, if you wish) and blend until smooth.

Pass the mixture through a sieve into a large saucepan, discard the seeds and pulp left in the sieve and bring to a boil. As soon as the mixture begins to boil, stir in the arrowroot mixture to thicken the liquid. Remove from the heat and stir in the vanilla and alcohol.

Chill in the fridge until cold and churn.

Transfer the ice cream to a freezer-safe container and freeze for at least 3 hours or overnight.

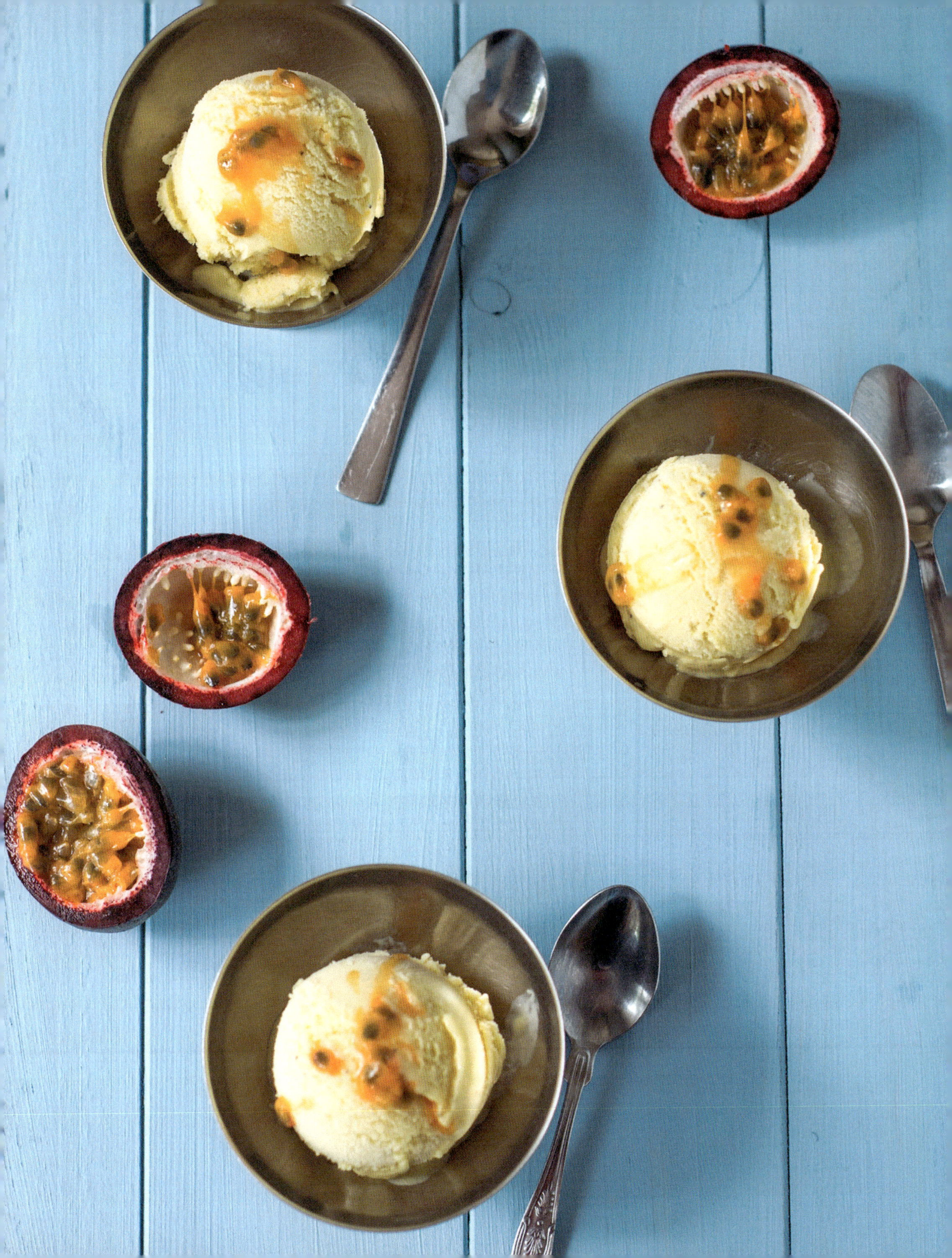

Roasted Pineapple

Yields approx 2 pints / 1 quart

If you've never had roasted pineapple before, I urge you to try it. It's a dessert in itself but is most delicious in this ice cream.

720ml / 3 cups coconut milk
2 tbsp arrowroot powder
1 medium pineapple, skin removed
2 tbsp coconut sugar
1 tbsp coconut oil
120ml / ½ cup maple syrup
1 tsp vanilla extract
(optional) 1 tbsp alcohol

Preheat the oven to 180°C / 350°F. Mix 60ml / ¼ cup coconut milk with the arrowroot powder in a small bowl and set aside.

Chop the pineapple into small chunks and place in a small roasting tin with the coconut sugar and coconut oil. Gently toss to make sure it's evenly coated and roast for 15-20 minutes until it begins to turn brown.

Take half of the roasted pineapple, put it in a bowl and refrigerate it for later. Put the other half in a blender and mix with the rest of the coconut milk and the maple syrup. Mix until smooth and pour into a large saucepan. Bring to a boil and stir in the arrowroot mixture to thicken the liquid. Remove from the heat and stir in the vanilla and alcohol.

Chill the mixture in the fridge until cold and churn. During the last few minutes of churning, add the rest of the roasted pineapple chunks.

Transfer the ice cream to a freezer-safe container and freeze for at least 3 hours or overnight.

Papaya & Lime

Yields approx 2 pints / 1 quart

The acid from the lime really brings out the flavour and sweetness of the papaya. In fact, I don't eat papaya without it!

720ml / 3 cups coconut milk
2 tbsp arrowroot powder
2 medium papayas, peeled & de-seeded
Juice of 1 lime
120ml / ½ cup maple syrup
1 tsp vanilla extract
(optional) 1 tbsp alcohol

Mix 60ml / ¼ cup coconut milk with the arrowroot powder in a small bowl and set aside.

Slice the papaya and place it in a blender with the rest of the coconut milk, the lime juice and the maple syrup. Mix until smooth.

Pour the mixture into a large saucepan and bring to a boil. As soon as the mixture begins to boil, stir in the arrowroot mixture to thicken the liquid. Remove from the heat and stir in the vanilla and alcohol.

Chill the mixture in the fridge until cold and churn.

Transfer the ice cream to a freezer-safe container and freeze for at least 3 hours or overnight.

Roasted Plum & Cardamom

Yields approx 2 pints / 1 quart

The fragrant cardamom really lifts the flavour of what would have been an ordinary fruity ice cream. The coconut milk works great in this recipe as it's soothing taste and texture mellows these strong flavours, just the right amount.

720ml / 3 cups coconut milk
2 tbsp arrowroot powder
15 cardamom pods, crushed
10 plums, halved and pitted
2 tbsp coconut sugar
1 tbsp lemon juice
½ tsp ground cardamom
120ml / ½ cup maple syrup
1 tsp vanilla extract
(optional) 1 tbsp alcohol

Mix 60ml / ¼ cup coconut milk with the arrowroot powder in a small bowl and set aside to thicken.

Pour the rest of the coconut milk into a saucepan with the crushed cardamom pods and bring to a simmer. Remove from the heat and let the pods steep in the milk for at least 1 hour.

Preheat the oven to 190°C / 370°F. Place the plums on a lined baking sheet, sprinkle over the coconut sugar and lemon juice and roast for 20-25 minutes until the plums are soft and tender.

Strain the milk and discard the pods. Add the milk to a blender along with the plums, ground cardamom and maple syrup. Blend until smooth and transfer to a saucepan. Bring the mixture to a boil then immediately stir in the arrowroot mixture to thicken the liquid. Remove from the heat and stir in the vanilla and alcohol.

Chill in the fridge until cold, then churn.

Transfer the ice cream to a freezer-safe container and freeze for at least 3 hours or overnight.

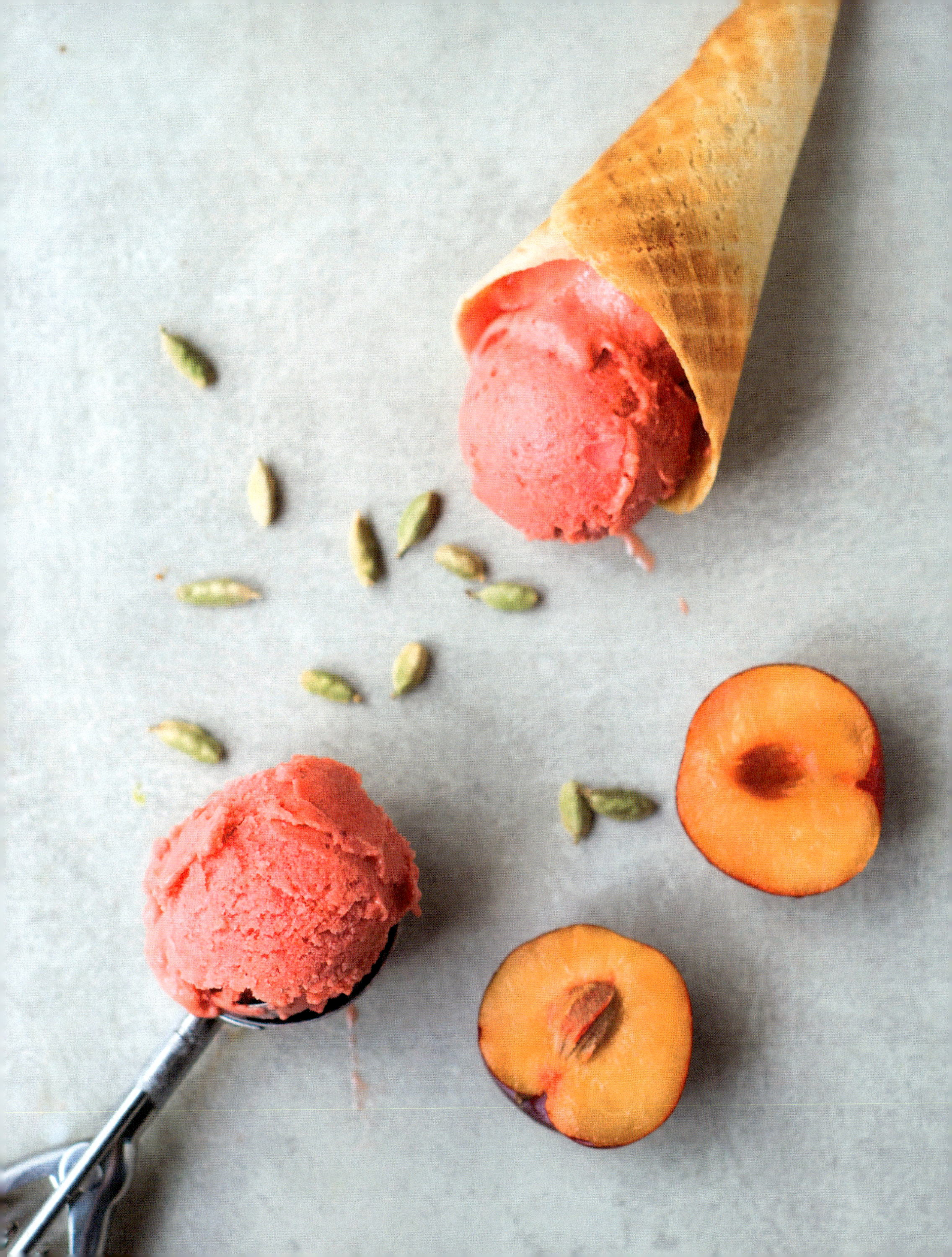

Pomegranate

Yields approx 2 pints / 1 quart

A light pink ice cream with a fragrant, fruity taste. Decorate with fresh pomegranate seeds for a beautiful dessert.

720ml / 3 cups coconut milk
2 tbsp arrowroot powder
240ml / 1 cup pomegranate juice*
120ml / ½ cup maple syrup
1 tsp vanilla extract
(optional) 1 tbsp alcohol

*If you're making your own pomegranate juice, reserve some of the seeds for decoration

Mix 60ml / ¼ cup coconut milk with the arrowroot powder in a small bowl and set aside.

Pour the rest of the coconut milk, the pomegranate juice and maple syrup into a large saucepan and bring to a boil. As soon as the mixture begins to boil, stir in the arrowroot mixture to thicken the liquid. Remove from the heat and stir in the vanilla and alcohol.

Chill the mixture in the fridge until cold and churn.

Transfer the ice cream to a freezer-safe container and freeze for at least 3 hours or overnight.

Sweet Melon

Yields approx 2 pints / 1 quart

So sweet, so refreshing. Perfect for when you're feeling parched and need a "sugar hit" at the same time.

720ml / 3 cups coconut milk
2 tbsp arrowroot powder
½ a ripe cantaloupe
120ml / ½ cup maple syrup
1 tsp vanilla extract
(optional) 1 tbsp alcohol

Mix 60ml / ¼ cup coconut milk with the arrowroot powder in a small bowl and set aside.

Chop the cantaloupe into chunks and put in a blender with the rest of the coconut milk and the maple syrup. Mix until smooth then pour the mixture into a large saucepan and bring to a boil. As soon as the mixture begins to boil, stir in the arrowroot mixture to thicken the liquid. Remove from the heat and stir in the vanilla and alcohol.

Chill the mixture in the fridge until cold and churn.

Transfer the ice cream to a freezer-safe container and freeze for at least 3 hours or overnight.

COCONUT MILK ICE CREAM

Date

Yields approx 2 pints / 1 quart

This ice cream needs no added sugar as the dates provide all the sweetness you need! You could try using this as a healthy base ice cream recipe and adding other ingredients to make different flavours.

720ml / 3 cups coconut milk
2 tbsp arrowroot powder
120ml / ½ cup water
175g / 1 cup chopped and pitted dates
1 tsp vanilla extract (optional) 1 tbsp alcohol

Mix 60ml / ¼ cup coconut milk with the arrowroot powder in a small bowl and set aside.

Boil the water and pour it into a bowl with the dates. Let it soak for about an hour. When it's cooled, process the water and dates together in a food processor or high-powered blender until it creates a purée. Add a bit of coconut milk, if needed.

Add the purée to a large saucepan with the rest of the coconut milk and bring to a boil. As soon as the mixture begins to boil, stir in the arrowroot mixture to thicken the liquid. Remove from the heat and stir in the vanilla and alcohol.

Chill the mixture in the fridge until cold and churn. Transfer the ice cream to a freezer-safe container and freeze for at least 3 hours or overnight.

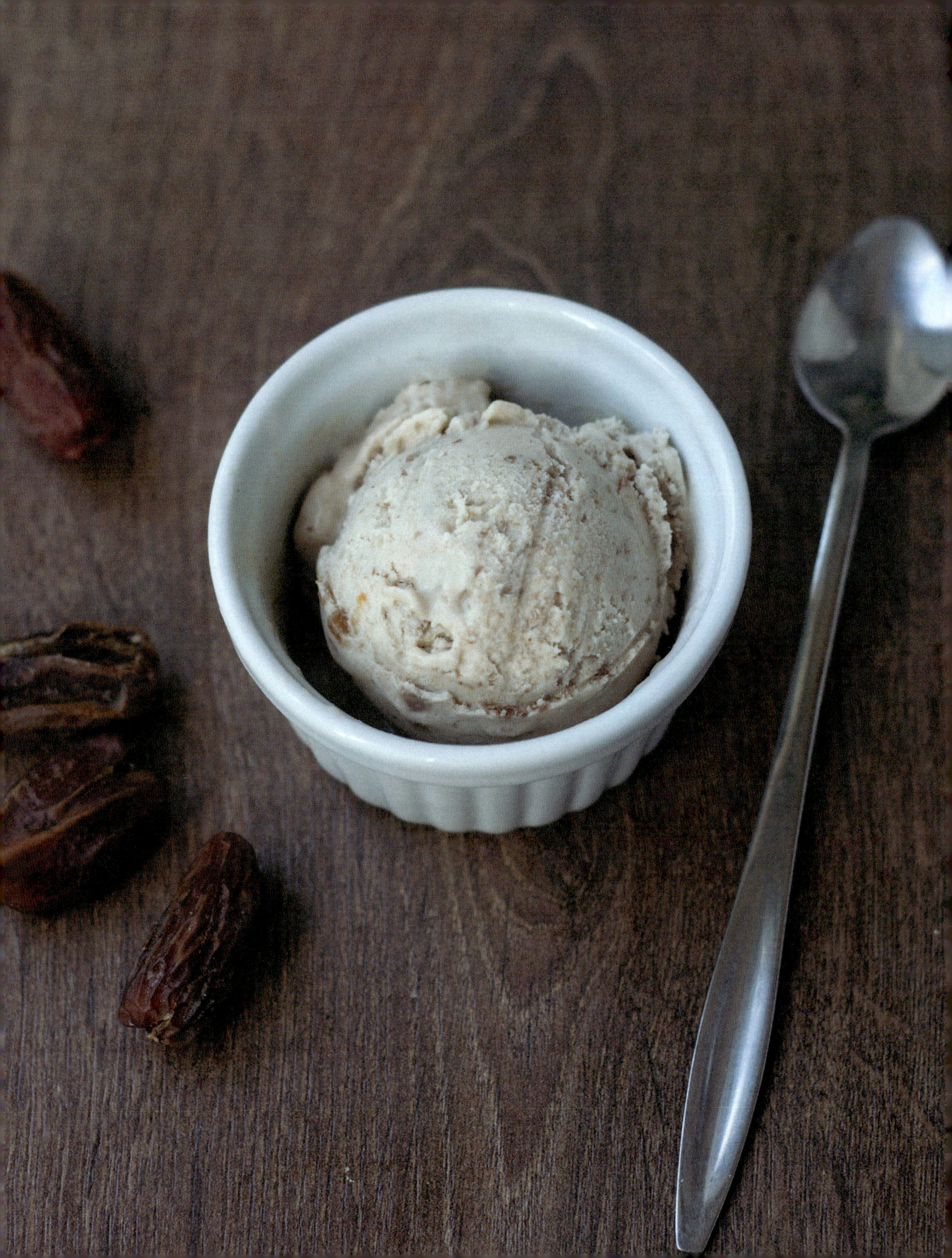

Strawberry

Yields approx 2 pints / 1 quart

You can't beat strawberry ice cream made with real strawberries. They can be swapped for blackberries, raspberries or other berries to make different flavours.

720ml / 3 cups coconut milk
2 tbsp arrowroot powder
125g / 1 cup strawberries
120ml / ½ cup maple syrup
1 tsp vanilla extract
(optional) 1 tbsp alcohol

Mix 60ml / ¼ cup coconut milk with the arrowroot powder in a small bowl and set aside.

Hull and slice the strawberries and place them in a blender with the rest of the coconut milk and maple syrup. Mix until smooth.

Pour the mixture into a large saucepan and bring to a boil. As soon as the mixture begins to boil, stir in the arrowroot mixture to thicken the liquid. Remove from the heat and stir in the vanilla and alcohol.

Chill the mixture in the fridge until cold and churn.

Transfer the ice cream to a freezer-safe container and freeze for at least 3 hours or overnight.

COCONUT MILK ICE CREAM

Caramelized Banana

Yields approx 2 pints / 1 quart

This ice cream is a great way to use up old bananas and doesn't require much extra sugar as the bananas provide most of the sweetness.

720ml / 3 cups coconut milk
2 tbsp arrowroot powder
6-7 medium *very* ripe bananas, chopped
45g / ⅓ cup coconut sugar
Pinch of salt
1 tsp vanilla extract
(optional) 1 tbsp alcohol

Mix 60ml / ¼ cup coconut milk with the arrowroot powder in a small bowl and set aside to thicken.

Pour another ¼ cup of the coconut milk into a large saucepan and add the bananas, coconut sugar and salt. Bring to a medium heat and cook until the bananas turn mushy. Add the mixture to a blender along with the rest of the coconut milk and blend until smooth. Return to the saucepan.

Bring the mixture to a boil then immediately add the arrowroot mixture. Stir for another couple of minutes until the mixture thickens noticeably. Remove from heat and stir in the vanilla alcohol.

Chill in the fridge until cold and churn.

Transfer the ice cream to a freezer-safe container and freeze for at least 3 hours or overnight.

COCONUT MILK ICE CREAM

Peaches & Cream

Yields approx 2 pints / 1 quart

Peaches and cream are a well loved combination for a reason. This ice cream makes a refreshing yet comforting summertime treat.

720ml / 3 cups coconut milk
2 tbsp arrowroot powder
7-8 peaches, peeled and pitted
120ml / ½ cup maple syrup
2 tsp vanilla extract
(optional) 1 tbsp alcohol

Mix 60ml / ¼ cup coconut milk with the arrowroot powder in a small bowl and set aside to thicken.

Slice the peaches and add them to a saucepan with 1 tbsp of the maple syrup. Cook on a low heat until softened, then mash into a thick purée. Transfer to a bowl or container and leave to cool in the fridge.

Pour the rest of the coconut milk and maple syrup into a saucepan and bring to a boil. As soon as the mixture begins to boil, stir in the arrowroot mixture to thicken the liquid. Remove from the heat and stir in the vanilla and alcohol.

Chill the mixture in the fridge until cold and churn. During the last minute of churning, add the peach purée so it creates a rippled effect.

Transfer the ice cream to a freezer-safe container and freeze for at least 3 hours or overnight.

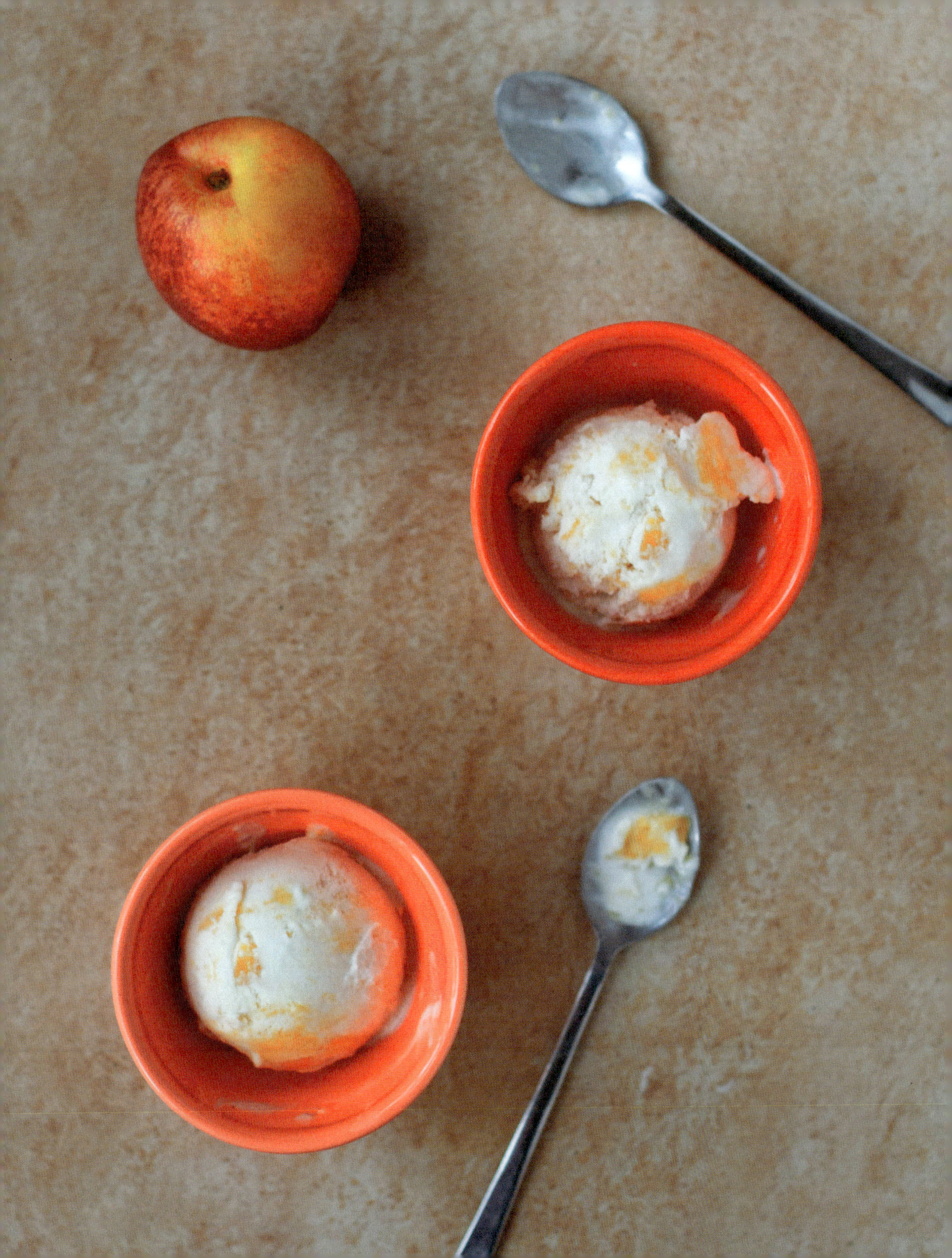

Orange

Yields approx 2 pints / 1 quart

Zesty, refreshing and totally mood uplifting. Get a vitamin C boost with this delicious Orange Ice Cream.

720ml / 3 cups coconut milk
2 tbsp arrowroot powder
3 tbsp zest and 1 cup of juice from 2-3 large oranges
120ml / ½ cup maple syrup
1 tsp vanilla extract
(optional) 1 tbsp alcohol

Mix 60ml / ¼ cup coconut milk with the arrowroot powder in a small bowl and set aside to thicken.

Pour the rest of the coconut milk with the orange juice, zest and maple syrup into a large saucepan and bring to a boil. As soon as the mixture begins to boil stir in the arrowroot mixture to thicken the liquid.

Remove from the heat and stir in the vanilla and alcohol.

Chill the mixture in the fridge until cold and churn.

Transfer the ice cream to a freezer-safe container and freeze for at least 3 hours or overnight.

Apricot

Yields approx 2 pints / 1 quart

Similar to peaches, apricots have a really light, almost floral but a little musky taste to them. You can add some dried apricots to this ice cream for some added texture and sweetness.

720ml / 3 cups coconut milk
2 tbsp arrowroot powder
4 apricots, peeled, pitted and chopped
120ml / ½ cup maple syrup
1 tsp vanilla extract
(optional) 1 tbsp alcohol
(optional) 40g / ¼ cup dried apricots, chopped into small chunks

Mix 60ml / ¼ cup coconut milk with the arrowroot powder in a small bowl and set aside.

Put the apricots in a blender with the rest of the coconut milk and the maple syrup. Mix until smooth then pour the mixture into a large saucepan and bring to a boil. As soon as the mixture begins to boil, stir in the arrowroot mixture to thicken the liquid. Remove from the heat and stir in the vanilla and alcohol.

Chill the mixture in the fridge until cold and churn. (Optional) during the last few minutes of churning, add the dried apricots.

Transfer the ice cream to a freezer-safe container and freeze for at least 3 hours or overnight.

COCONUT MILK ICE CREAM

NUT & SEED FLAVOURS

Pecan Praline..55
Peanut Butter Chocolate Swirl...............56
Pistachio..58
Chestnut Caramel.....................................59
Chocolate Hazelnut..................................60
Maple Glazed Walnut..............................62
Salted Almonds...63
Toasted Sesame Seed..............................64

Pecan Praline

Yields approx 2 pints / 1 quart

Smooth ice cream with crunchy, sweet, nutty praline. Heaven!

For the pecan praline:
65g / ½ cup chopped caramelized pecan nuts (see page 151)

For the ice cream:
720ml / 3 cups coconut milk
2 tbsp arrowroot powder
120ml / ½ cup maple syrup
½ tsp almond extract
1 tsp vanilla extract
(optional) 1 tbsp alcohol

Mix 60ml / ¼ cup coconut milk with the arrowroot powder in a small bowl and set aside to thicken.

Pour the rest of the coconut milk and maple syrup into a large saucepan and bring to a boil. As soon as the mixture begins to boil, stir in the arrowroot mixture to thicken the liquid. Remove from the heat and stir in the almond extract, vanilla and alcohol.

Chill the mixture in the fridge until cold and churn. During the last few minutes of churning, add the pecan praline pieces.

Transfer the ice cream to a freezer-safe container and freeze for at least 3 hours or overnight.

COCONUT MILK ICE CREAM

Peanut Butter Chocolate Swirl

Yields approx 2 pints / 1 quart

A favourite flavour combination in ice cream form. Add some salted peanuts on top for a nice crunch.

For the ice cream:
720ml / 3 cups coconut milk
2 tbsp arrowroot powder
120ml / ½ cup maple syrup
1 tsp vanilla extract
(optional) 1 tbsp alcohol

For the chocolate peanut sauce:
45g / ¼ cup dark chocolate chips
65g / ¼ cup peanut butter

To serve:
Chopped salted peanuts

Make the chocolate peanut sauce by gently melting the chocolate chips in a heat proof bowl over a simmering pot of water. Stir in the peanut butter and mix well until you have a thick sauce. Leave to cool at room temperature.

Mix 60ml / ¼ cup coconut milk with the arrowroot powder in a small bowl and set aside to thicken.

Pour the rest of the milk into a saucepan with the maple syrup and bring to a boil, immediately stir in the arrowroot mixture to thicken the liquid. Remove from the heat and stir in the vanilla and alcohol.

Chill in the fridge until cold, then churn.

Transfer the mixture to a freezer-safe container. Pour the sauce over the ice cream and use a skewer to swirl it through.

Freeze for at least 3 hours or overnight.

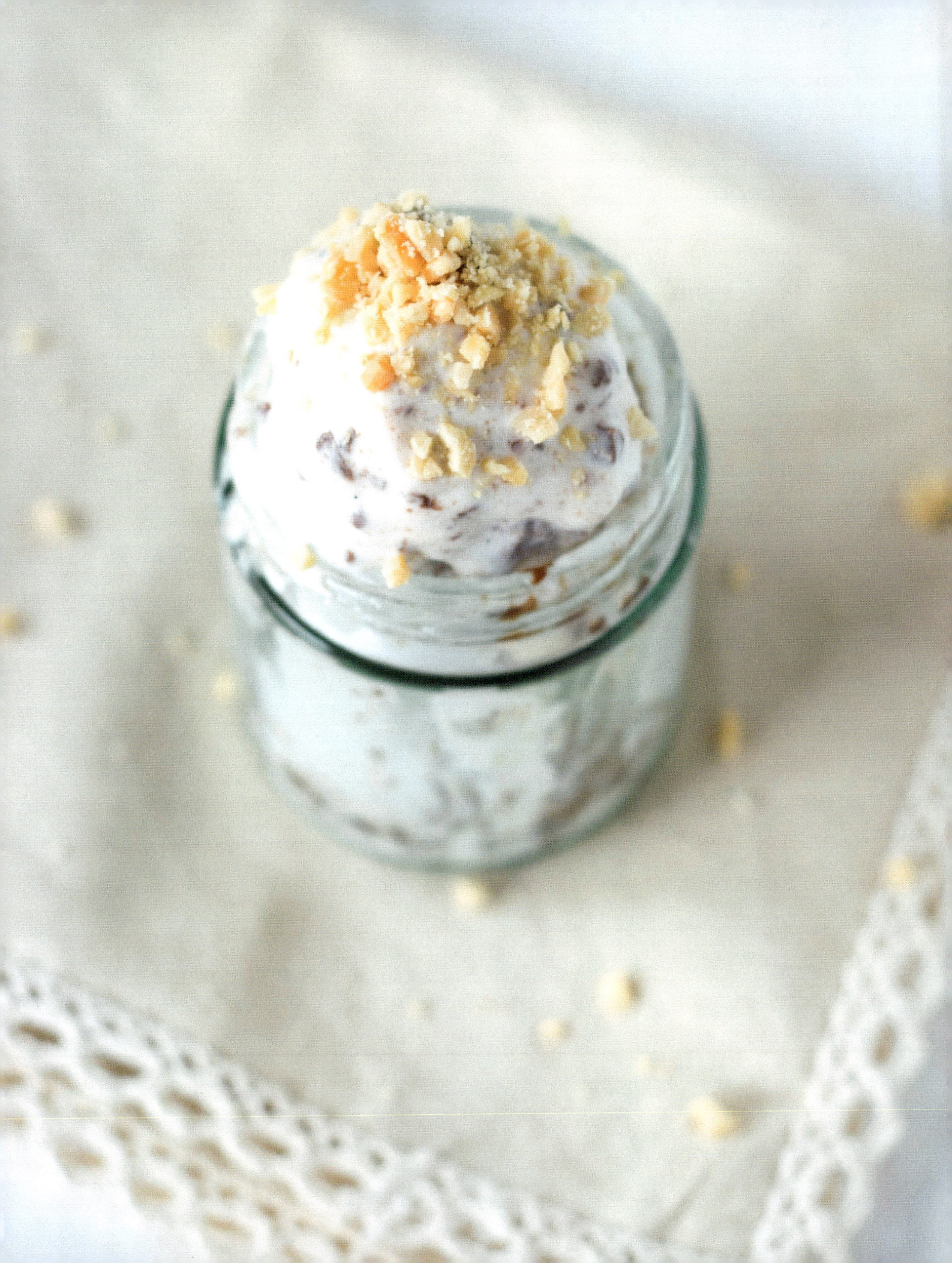

Pistachio

Yields approx 2 pints / 1 quart

I love the pale green colour and the crunchy, salty nuttiness of this pistachio ice cream.

720ml / 3 cups coconut milk
2 tbsp arrowroot powder
115g / 1 cup pistachios, chopped
A pinch of salt
120ml / ½ cup maple syrup
1 tsp vanilla extract
(optional) 1 tbsp alcohol

Mix 60ml / ¼ cup coconut milk with the arrowroot powder in a small bowl and set aside.

Mix ¾ cup of the pistachios (save the rest for topping) in a food processor until ground.

Pour the rest of the coconut milk into a blender with the ground pistachios, salt and the maple syrup. Blend until as smooth as possible.

Pour the mixture into a saucepan and bring to a boil. As soon as the mixture begins to boil, stir in the arrowroot mixture to thicken the liquid. Remove from the heat and stir in the vanilla and alcohol.

Chill the mixture in the fridge until cold and churn.

Transfer the ice cream to a freezer-safe container and freeze for at least 3 hours or overnight. Top with the leftover chopped pistachios.

Chestnut Caramel

Yields approx 2 pints / 1 quart

A smooth and very indulgent treat that would be delicious any time of the year. If you want to serve it at Christmas time, try adding a pinch of cinnamon.

720ml / 3 cups coconut milk
2 tbsp arrowroot powder
115g / ½ cup chestnut puree
140g / 1 cup coconut sugar*
A pinch of salt
2 tsp vanilla extract
(optional) 1 tbsp alcohol

*Make sure you use coconut sugar and not palm sugar

Mix 60ml / ¼ cup coconut milk with the arrowroot powder in a small bowl and set aside.

Pour the rest of the coconut milk into a large saucepan with the chestnut puree, coconut sugar and salt. As soon as the mixture begins to boil, stir in the stir in the arrowroot mixture to thicken the liquid. Remove from the heat and stir in the vanilla and alcohol.

Chill in the fridge until cold and churn.

Transfer the ice cream to a freezer-safe container and freeze for at least 3 hours or overnight.

COCONUT MILK ICE CREAM

Chocolate Hazelnut

Yields approx 2 pints / 1 quart

This ice cream is one for the Nutella fans! Delicious served in a chocolate-dipped waffle cone with chopped roasted hazelnuts on top.

720ml / 3 cups coconut milk
2 tbsp arrowroot powder
120ml / ½ cup maple syrup
2 tbsp hazelnut butter
2 tbsp cocoa powder
1 tsp vanilla
(optional) 1 tbsp alcohol

For the chocolate hazelnut sauce:
45g / ¼ cup dark chocolate chips
65g / ¼ cup hazelnut butter

Make the chocolate hazelnut sauce by gently melting the chocolate in a heat proof bowl over a pot of simmering water. Stir in the hazelnut butter and mix well until you have a thick sauce. Leave to cool at room temperature.

Mix 60ml / ¼ cup coconut milk with the arrowroot powder in a small bowl and set aside to thicken.

Pour the rest of the coconut milk into a blender with the maple syrup, hazelnut butter and cocoa powder and blend until smooth. Pour into a saucepan and bring to a boil, immediately stir in the arrowroot mixture to thicken the liquid. Remove from the heat and stir in the vanilla and alcohol.

Chill in the fridge until cold, then churn.

When the ice cream has churned, transfer the mixture to a freezer-safe container. Pour the sauce over the ice cream and use a skewer to swirl it through.

Freeze for at least 3 hours or overnight.

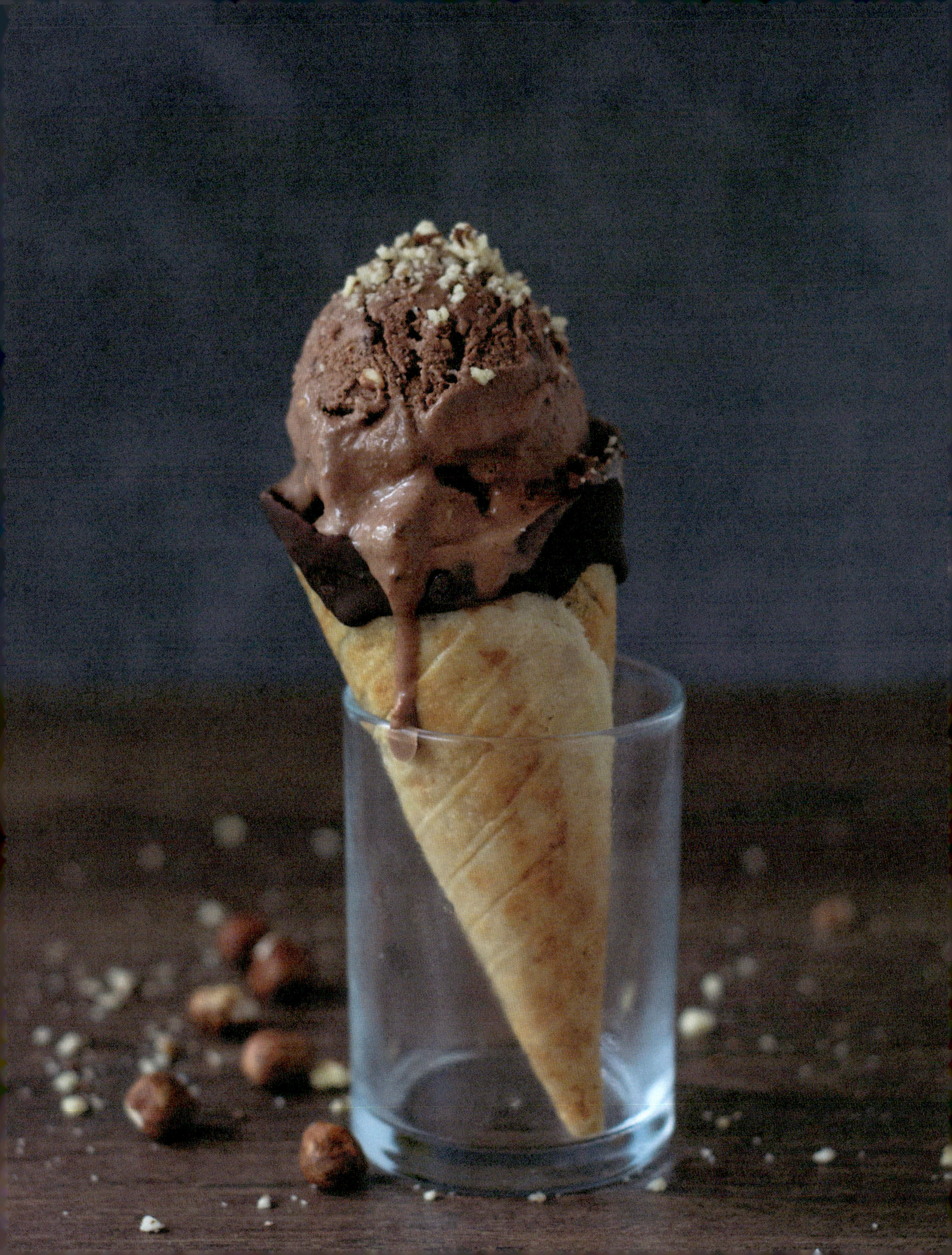

Maple Glazed Walnut

Yields approx 2 pints / 1 quart

Maple and walnuts make such a great pair, highlighted by this sweet, nutty ice cream.

720ml / 3 cups coconut milk
2 tbsp arrowroot powder
120ml / ½ cup maple syrup
1 tsp vanilla extract
(optional) 1 tbsp alcohol
65g / ½ cup chopped caramelized walnuts (see page 151)

Mix 60ml / ¼ cup coconut milk with the arrowroot powder in a small bowl and set aside.

Pour the rest of the coconut milk into a saucepan with the maple syrup and bring to a boil. As soon as the mixture begins to boil, stir in the arrowroot mixture to thicken the liquid. Remove from the heat and stir in the vanilla and alcohol.

Chill the mixture in the fridge until cold and churn. Add the glazed walnuts in the last few minutes of churning.

Transfer the ice cream to a freezer-safe container and freeze for at least 3 hours or overnight.

Salted Almonds

Yields approx 2 pints / 1 quart

If you love sweet and salty combinations, you'll love this ice cream. I was tempted to substitute some of the coconut milk for almond milk here but didn't want to compromise on the quality of the ice cream. The almond extract and chopped almonds add all the almond flavour you'll need!

720ml / 3 cups coconut milk
2 tbsp arrowroot powder
120ml / ½ cup maple syrup
1 tsp almond extract
1 tsp vanilla extract
(optional) 1 tbsp alcohol
65g / ½ cup caramelized almond nuts (see page 151)
½ tsp of salt

Mix 60ml / ¼ cup coconut milk with the arrowroot powder in a small bowl and set aside.

Pour the rest of the coconut milk into a saucepan with the rest of the maple syrup and bring to a boil. As soon as the mixture begins to boil, stir in the arrowroot mixture to thicken the liquid. Remove from the heat and stir in the almond extract, vanilla and alcohol.

Chill the mixture in the fridge until cold and churn. Salt the caramelized almonds and add them to the ice cream in the last few minutes of churning.

Transfer the ice cream to a freezer-safe container and freeze for at least 3 hours or overnight.

COCONUT MILK ICE CREAM

Toasted Sesame Seed

Yields approx 2 pints / 1 quart

I love the toasty, nuttiness offset by the sweetness of the ice cream. Very addictive.

720ml / 3 cups coconut milk
2 tbsp arrowroot powder
75g / ½ cup sesame seeds
1 tbsp tahini
120ml / ½ cup maple syrup
1 tsp vanilla extract
(optional) 1 tbsp alcohol

Mix 60ml / ¼ cup coconut milk with the arrowroot powder in a small bowl and set aside.

Heat a dry skillet and toast the sesame seeds, shaking the pan often to prevent burning. Toast until lightly golden and reserve approx 1 tbsp for serving later on. Pour the rest into a large saucepan.

Pour the rest of the coconut milk and tahini into the saucepan with the sesame seeds. Bring to a boil then remove from the heat and let the toasted sesame seeds infuse the milk for at least 1 hour.

Pour the milk through a sieve into a large saucepan and discard the seeds. Add the maple syrup and bring the mixture to a boil again, then stir in the arrowroot mixture. Remove from the heat and stir in the vanilla and alcohol.

Chill the mixture in the fridge until cold and churn. Transfer the ice cream to a shallow freezer-safe container and freeze for at least 3 hours or overnight. Sprinkle the reserved sesame seeds on top for decoration.

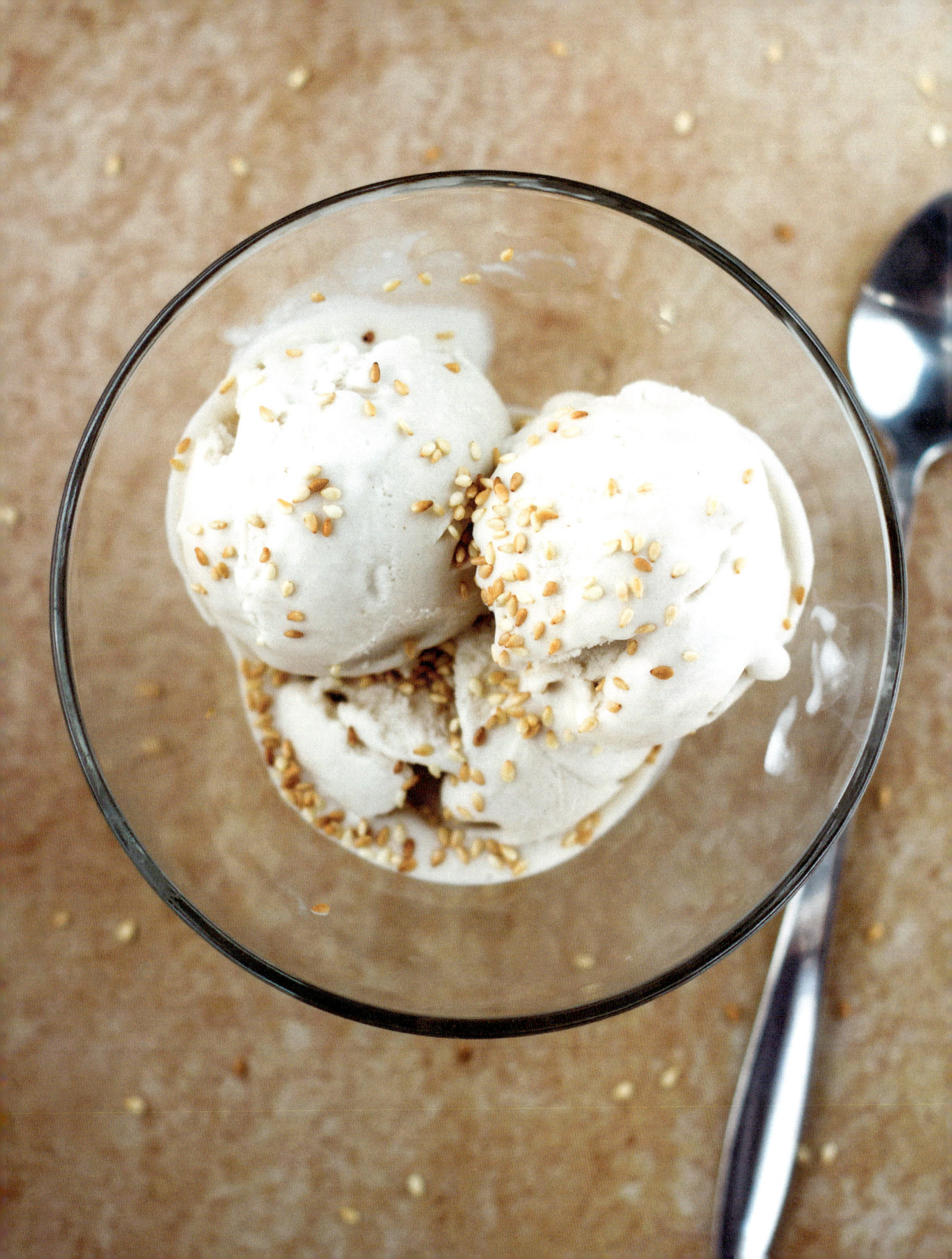

SPICY FLAVOURS

Fresh Ginger....................................67
Mayan Chocolate............................68
Wasabi...70
Chinese Five-Spice.........................71
Sweet Curry....................................72

Fresh Ginger

Yields approx 2 pints / 1 quart

Awaken your senses with the fresh zing and kick of ginger in this delicious ice cream.

720ml / 3 cups coconut milk
2 tbsp arrowroot powder
3 tbsp fresh ginger, grated
120ml / ½ cup maple syrup
1 tsp vanilla extract
(optional) 1 tbsp alcohol

Mix 60ml / ¼ cup coconut milk with the arrowroot powder in a small bowl and set aside.

Pour the rest of the coconut milk into a large saucepan with the fresh ginger and bring to a boil, stirring all the time. Remove from the heat and let the ingredients steep in the milk for about 30 minutes.

Sieve the mixture into a large saucepan, add the maple syrup and bring to the boil again. As soon as the mixture begins to boil, stir in the arrowroot mixture to thicken the liquid. Remove from the heat and stir in the vanilla and alcohol.

Chill the mixture in the fridge until cold and churn.

Transfer the ice cream to a freezer-safe container and freeze for at least 3 hours or overnight.

COCONUT MILK ICE CREAM

Mayan Chocolate

Yields approx 2 pints / 1 quart

A dark, luscious chocolate ice cream with a hot kick of cayenne pepper and a dash of sweet, warm cinnamon. One of my favourites.

720ml / 3 cups coconut milk
2 tbsp arrowroot powder
20g / ¼ cup cocoa powder
1 tsp ground cinnamon
⅓ tsp ground cayenne pepper*
A pinch of salt
120ml / ½ cup maple syrup
90g / ½ cup dark chocolate chips
(optional) 1 tbsp alcohol

*Add a tiny bit more if you like the heat!

Mix 60ml / ¼ cup coconut milk with the arrowroot powder in a small bowl and set aside.

Pour the rest of the coconut milk into a large saucepan with the cocoa powder, spices, salt and maple syrup and bring to a boil, stirring all the time. As soon as the mixture begins to boil, stir in the arrowroot mixture to thicken the liquid. Remove from the heat and stir in the chocolate chips and alcohol. Keep stirring until all the chocolate is melted.

Chill the mixture in the fridge until cold and churn.

Transfer the ice cream to a freezer-safe container and freeze for at least 3 hours or overnight.

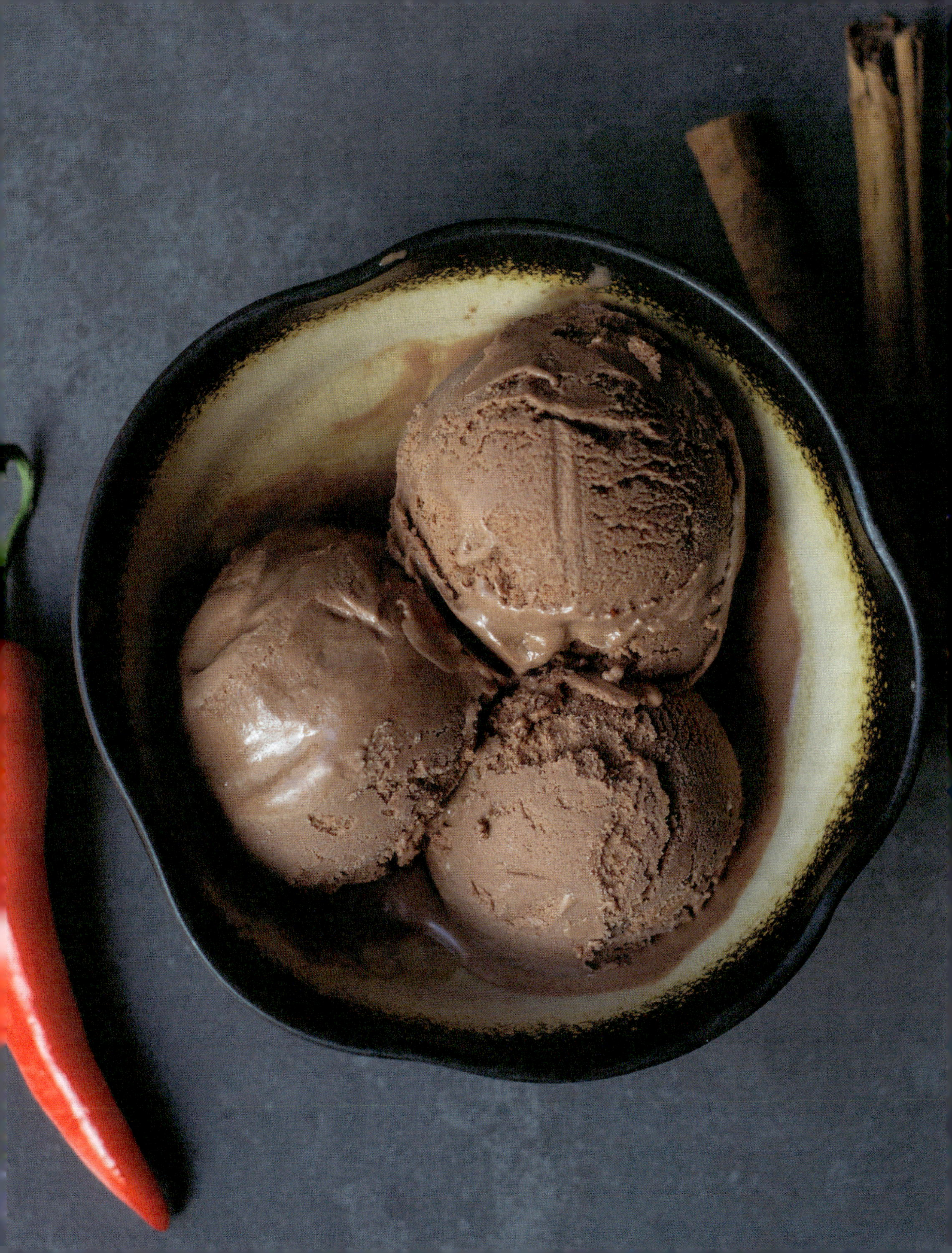

Wasabi

Yields approx 2 pints / 1 quart

Wait. Hear me out. I promise this ice cream won't blow your socks off, heat-wise. It has a wonderful taste and will help clear you sinuses.

720ml / 3 cups coconut milk
2 tbsp arrowroot powder
120ml / ½ cup maple syrup
½ tsp wasabi paste, or more depending on your taste
1 tsp vanilla extract
(optional) 1 tbsp alcohol

Mix 60ml / ¼ cup coconut milk with the arrowroot powder in a small bowl and set aside.

Pour the rest of the coconut milk into a large saucepan with the maple syrup and bring to a boil, stirring all the time. As soon as the mixture begins to boil, stir in the arrowroot mixture to thicken the liquid.

Remove from the heat and whisk in the wasabi, vanilla and alcohol until well combined. Taste and adjust spice if needed.

Chill the mixture in the fridge until cold and churn.

Transfer the ice cream to a freezer-safe container and freeze for at least 3 hours or overnight.

Chinese Five-Spice

Yields approx 2 pints / 1 quart

A warming and exotic ice cream that makes a comforting dessert. Perfect for even the winter months.

720ml / 3 cups coconut milk
2 tbsp arrowroot powder
1 star anise
10 cloves
½ tsp fennel seeds
¼ tsp cinnamon
Peel of one orange, chopped
1 tsp fresh grated ginger
120ml / ½ cup maple syrup
1 tsp vanilla extract
(optional) 1 tbsp alcohol

Mix 60ml / ¼ cup coconut milk with the arrowroot powder in a small bowl and set aside.

Pour the rest of the coconut milk into a large saucepan with the spices, orange peel and ginger and bring to a boil, stirring all the time. Remove from the heat and let the ingredients steep in the milk for about 30 minutes.

Sieve the mixture into a large saucepan, add the maple syrup and bring to the boil again. As soon as the mixture begins to boil, stir in the arrowroot mixture to thicken the liquid. Remove from the heat and stir in the vanilla and alcohol.

Chill the mixture in the fridge until cold and churn.

Transfer the ice cream to a freezer-safe container and freeze for at least 3 hours or overnight.

COCONUT MILK ICE CREAM

Sweet Curry

Yields approx 2 pints / 1 quart

A sweet treat for curry-lovers. Delicious served with Caramelized Cashews (see page 151)

720ml / 3 cups coconut milk
2 tbsp arrowroot powder
2 tsp Madras curry powder or a milder curry powder, if preferred
1 thumb sized piece of ginger, grated
120ml / ½ cup maple syrup (optional) 1 tbsp alcohol

Mix 60ml / ¼ cup coconut milk with the arrowroot powder in a small bowl and set aside.

Pour the rest of the coconut milk into a large saucepan with the curry powder and ginger and bring to a boil, stirring all the time. Remove from the heat and let the spices infuse the milk for about an hour.

Sieve the mixture into a large saucepan, add the maple syrup and bring to the boil again. As soon as the mixture begins to boil, stir in the arrowroot mixture to thicken the liquid. Remove from the heat and stir in the alcohol.

Chill the mixture in the fridge until cold and churn.

Transfer the ice cream to a freezer-safe container and freeze for at least 3 hours or overnight.

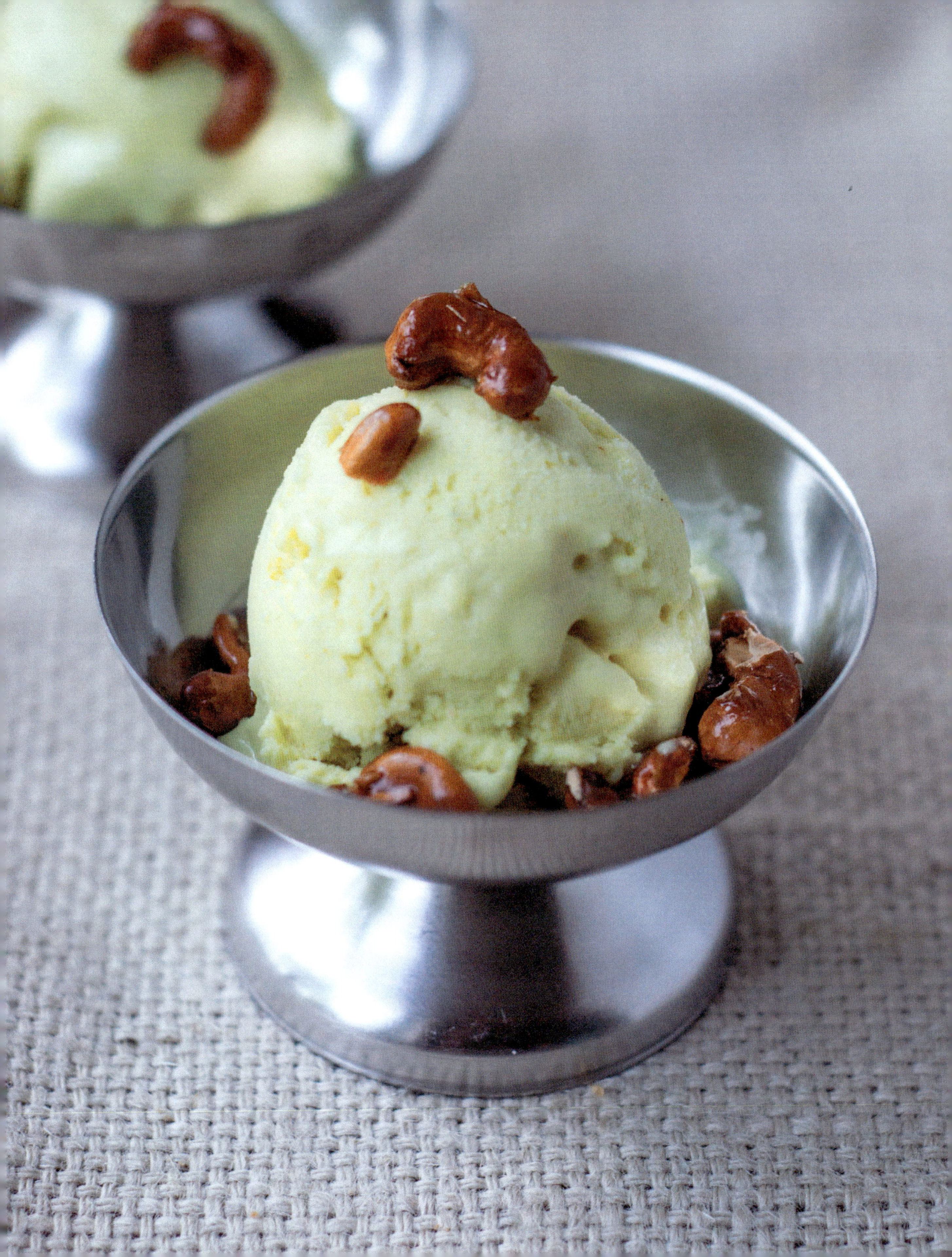

DESSERT INSPIRED FLAVOURS

Rhubarb Almond Crumble..................75
Lemon Poppy Seed Muffin..................76
Pumpkin Pie...78
Apple Pie...79
Red Velvet Beetroot Cake....................80
Coffee & Walnut Cake..........................82
Christmas Pudding...............................83

Rhubarb Almond Crumble

Yields approx 2 pints / 1 quart

Rhubarb crumble is one of my favourite desserts and I always make it with ground almonds, topped with flaked almonds. This ice cream captures that flavour and doesn't miss out on the crunch either, thanks to the flaked almond topping!

120g / 1 cup rhubarb, chopped
1 tbsp coconut sugar
1 tbsp lemon juice
720ml / 3 cups coconut milk
2 tbsp arrowroot powder
35g / ⅓ cup ground almonds
½ tsp ground cinnamon
(optional) 1 tsp beet powder, for colour
120ml / ½ cup maple syrup
1 tsp vanilla extract
(optional) 1 tbsp alcohol

To serve:
Flaked almonds

Preheat the oven to 180°C / 350°F. Place the rhubarb on a roasting tin, sprinkle the sugar and drizzle the lemon juice on top. Cover with tin foil and cook for 30 minutes until tender. Give the tin a shake half way through. Leave to cool.

Mix 60ml / ¼ cup coconut milk with the arrowroot powder in a small bowl and set aside to thicken.

Pour the rest of the coconut milk into a blender with the rhubarb, ground almonds, cinnamon, beet powder (if using) and maple syrup. Blend until smooth.

Pour the mixture into a large saucepan and bring to a boil. As soon as the mixture begins to boil stir in the arrowroot mixture to thicken. Remove from the heat and stir in the vanilla and alcohol.

Chill the mixture in the fridge until cold and churn.

Transfer the ice cream to a freezer-safe container and freeze for at least 3 hours or overnight. Serve with flaked almonds on top.

COCONUT MILK ICE CREAM

Lemon Poppy Seed Muffin

Yields approx 2 pints / 1 quart

My favourite type of muffin and my favourite ice cream in this book! This ice cream is exactly what you'd hope it to be - it's all the flavour of a poppy seed muffin in the form of ice cream.

720ml / 3 cups coconut milk
2 tbsp arrowroot powder
Zest and juice of 1 large lemon
120ml / ½ cup maple syrup
(optional) ¼ tsp turmeric
1 tsp vanilla extract
(optional) 1 tbsp alcohol
2 tbsp poppy seeds

variation: swap poppy seeds for chia seeds to add a superfood boost to this ice cream

Mix 60ml / ¼ cup coconut milk with the arrowroot powder in a small bowl and set aside.

Pour the rest of the coconut milk into a blender with the lemon zest and juice and the maple syrup. Blend until smooth then pour into a saucepan.

Bring the mixture to a boil and immediately stir in the arrowroot mixture and the turmeric, for a boost of yellow colouring. Lower the heat and stir for a couple of minutes until thickened. Remove from the heat and stir in the vanilla and alcohol.

Chill in the fridge until cold, then churn. During churning, add the poppy seeds.

When the ice cream has churned, transfer the mixture to a freezer-safe container and freeze for at least 3 hours or overnight.

COCONUT MILK ICE CREAM

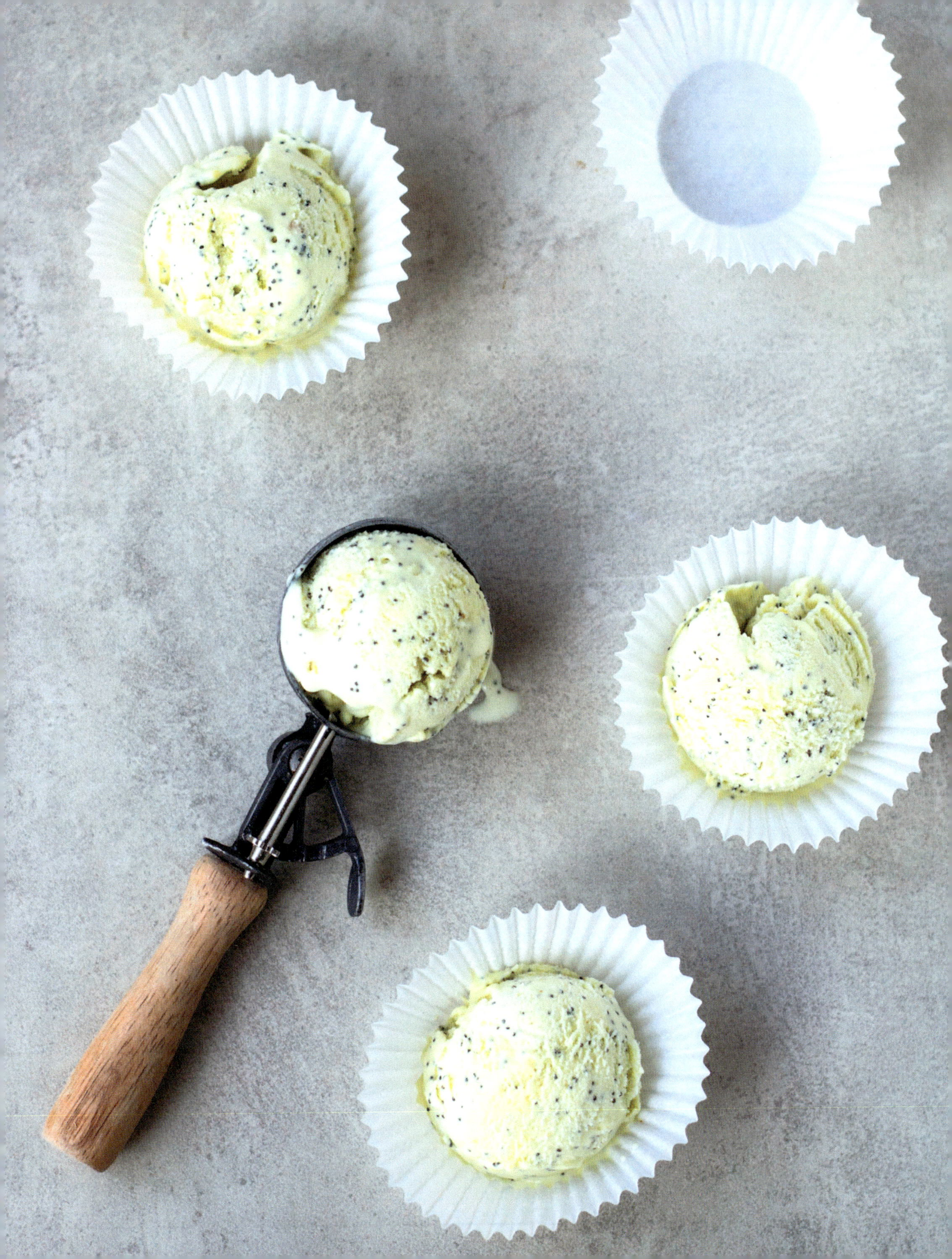

Pumpkin Pie

Yields approx 2 pints / 1 quart

A comforting, flavourful ice cream that makes a great alternative Thanksgiving or Christmas dessert.

720ml / 3 cups coconut milk
2 tbsp arrowroot powder
120ml / ½ cup maple syrup
165g / ¾ cup pumpkin purée
1 tsp ground cinnamon
½ tsp ground ginger
¼ tsp ground cloves
¼ tsp ground nutmeg
2 tsp vanilla extract
(optional) 1 tbsp alcohol

Mix 60ml / ¼ cup coconut milk with the arrowroot powder in a small bowl and set aside.

Mix the rest of the coconut milk with the maple syrup, pumpkin purée and spices in a blender. Blend until smooth.

Pour the mixture into a large saucepan and bring to a boil. As soon as the mixture begins to boil, stir in the arrowroot mixture to thicken the liquid. Remove from the heat and stir in the vanilla and alcohol.

Chill the mixture in the fridge until cold and churn.

Transfer the ice cream to a freezer-safe container and freeze for at least 3 hours or overnight.

COCONUT MILK ICE CREAM

Apple Pie

Yields approx 2 pints / 1 quart

A classic, warming dessert in the form of ice cream. Serve with caramel sauce for some extra indulgence! (See page 143)

---

2 large apples, peeled, cored and diced
1 tbsp lemon juice
2 tbsp coconut sugar
1 tsp ground cinnamon
¼ tsp ground nutmeg
¼ tsp ground cloves
720ml / 3 cups coconut milk
2 tbsp arrowroot powder
120ml / ½ cup maple syrup
1 tsp vanilla paste
(optional) 1 tbsp alcohol

Chop the apples into small chunks and add to a saucepan with 1 tbsp lemon juice. Stir in the sugar and spices and cook on a low heat for 15 minutes, until the apple has softened. Add a little water if it dries out.

Meanwhile, mix 60ml / ¼ cup coconut milk with the arrowroot powder in a small bowl and set aside.

Pour the rest of the coconut milk and the maple syrup into a blender and mix with the cooked apples. Blend until smooth.

Pour the mixture into saucepan and bring to a boil. As soon as the mixture begins to boil, immediately stir in the arrowroot mixture and then remove from the heat. Stir in the vanilla and alcohol.

Chill the mixture in the fridge until cold and churn.

Transfer the ice cream to a freezer-safe container and freeze for at least 3 hours or overnight.

COCONUT MILK ICE CREAM

Red Velvet Beetroot Cake

Yields approx 2 pints / 1 quart

The combination of beetroot and chocolate is usually approached with suspicion but is soon loved and devoured. This ice cream gives you a hit of chocolate with a subtle background flavour of the beetroot - as well as a gorgeous dark red velvet colour!

720ml / 3 cups coconut milk
2 tbsp arrowroot powder
210g / 1 cup roasted beetroot
120ml / ½ cup maple syrup
100g dark chocolate
1 tsp vanilla extract
(optional) 1 tbsp alcohol

Mix 60ml / ¼ cup coconut milk with the arrowroot powder in a small bowl and set aside to thicken.

Mix the beetroot and ¼ cup coconut milk in a blender until smooth. Pour through a strainer into a saucepan.

Pour in the rest of the coconut milk and maple syrup and bring to a boil, immediately stir in the arrowroot mixture, lower the heat and stir for another couple of seconds until thickened. Remove from the heat and stir in the chocolate and let it melt slowly, stirring occasionally. Once melted, stir in the vanilla and alcohol.

Chill in the fridge until cold, then churn.

When the ice cream has churned, transfer the mixture to a freezer-safe container and freeze for at least 3 hours or overnight.

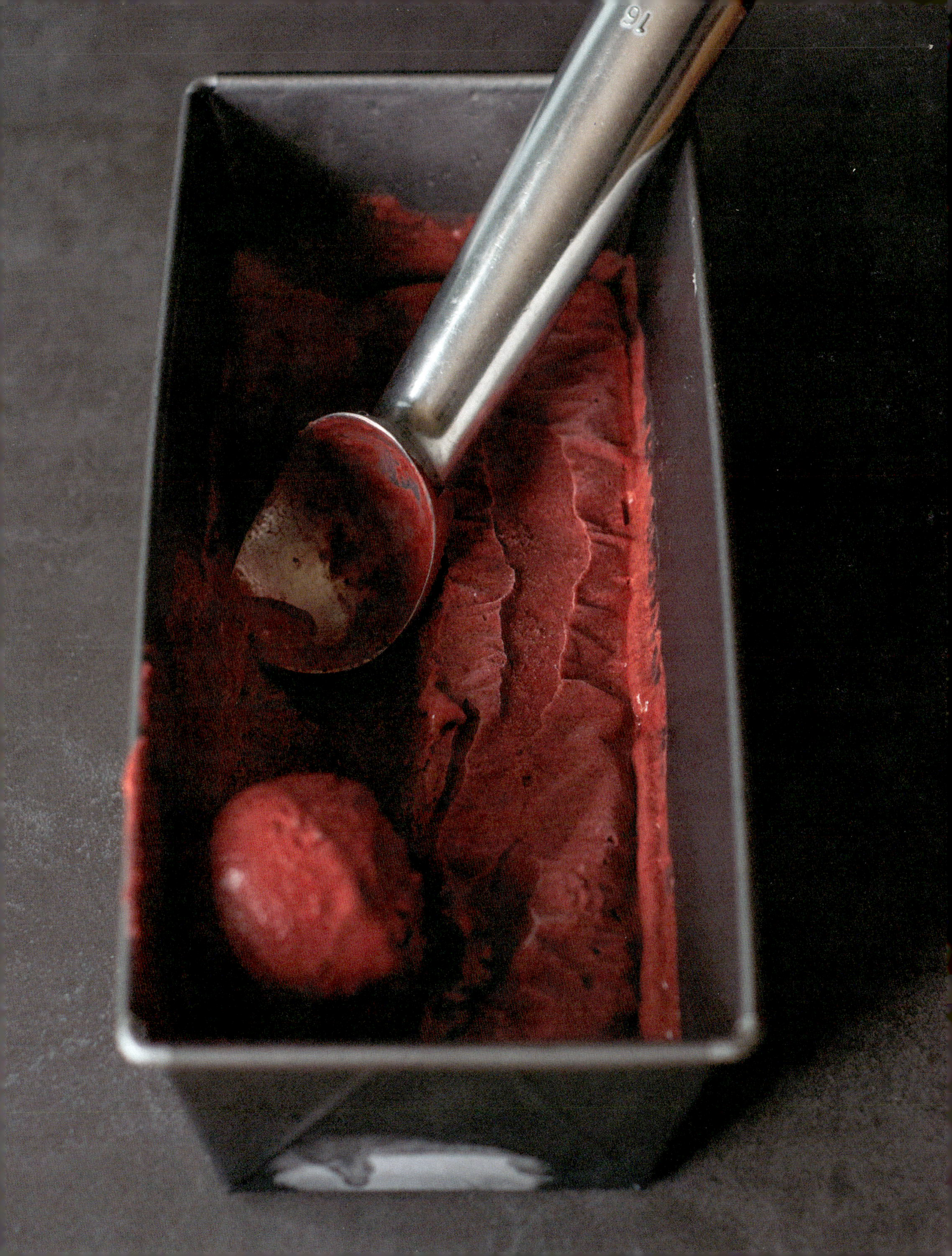

Coffee & Walnut Cake

Yields approx 2 pints / 1 quart

I love the strong, earthy and homely flavours of coffee & walnut. This ice cream will leave you feeling comforted and content.

720ml / 3 cups coconut milk
2 tbsp arrowroot powder
1 tbsp instant coffee
120ml / ½ cup maple syrup
2 tsp vanilla extract
65g / ½ cup chopped walnuts
(optional) 1 tbsp alcohol

Mix 60ml / ¼ cup coconut milk with the arrowroot powder in a small bowl and set aside.

Pour the rest of the coconut milk into a large saucepan with the maple syrup and coffee and bring to a boil. As soon as the mixture begins to boil, stir in the arrowroot mixture to thicken the liquid. Remove from the heat and stir in the vanilla and alcohol.

Chill the mixture in the fridge until cold and churn. During the last few minutes of churning, add the chopped walnuts.

Transfer the ice cream to a freezer-safe container and freeze for at least 3 hours or overnight.

COCONUT MILK ICE CREAM

Christmas Pudding

Yields approx 2 pints / 1 quart

This ice cream really does taste just like Christmas pudding! Serve scoops of the ice cream with holly leaves on top, for an alternative dessert at Christmas time.

720ml / 3 cups coconut milk
2 tbsp arrowroot powder
75g / ¼ cup molasses
35g / ⅓ cup ground almonds
50g / ¼ cup dried apricots, chopped
45g / ¼ cup dates, chopped
30g / ¼ cup cranberries
2 tsp cinnamon powder
1 tsp mixed spice (or pumpkin pie spice mix)
1 tbsp orange zest
1 tbsp lemon zest
1 tsp vanilla extract
(optional) 1 tbsp alcohol

Mix 60ml / ¼ cup coconut milk with the arrowroot powder in a small bowl and set aside. Reserve a tablespoon of each of the dried fruits for churning.

Pour ¾ cups of the coconut milk into a blender with the molasses, ground almonds, dried fruits, spices and zest. Blend until smooth and pour the mixture into a saucepan with the rest of the coconut milk.

Bring the mixture to a boil and stir in the arrowroot mixture to thicken the liquid. Remove from the heat and stir in the vanilla and alcohol.

Chill the mixture in the fridge until cold and churn. During the last few minutes of churning, add the reserved dried fruits.

Transfer the ice cream to a freezer-safe container and freeze for at least 3 hours or overnight.

COCONUT MILK ICE CREAM

BOOZY FLAVOURS

Pina Colada......................................85
Rum & Raisin....................................86
Apple Cider.....................................88
Irish Cream.....................................89
Roasted Cherry & Whiskey........................90
Mojito..92
White Wine......................................93

Pina Colada

Yields approx 2 pints / 1 quart

This Pina Colada ice cream would be great served at a cocktail party. You can dress it up with a mini umbrella and have a dessert and cocktail all in one!

720ml / 3 cups coconut milk
2 tbsp arrowroot powder
120ml / ½ cup maple syrup
160ml / ⅔ cup pineapple juice
120ml / ½ cup rum

Mix 60ml / ¼ cup coconut milk with the arrowroot powder in a small bowl and set aside.

Pour the rest of the coconut milk into a large saucepan with the maple syrup and pineapple juice and bring to a boil. As soon as the mixture begins to boil, stir in the arrowroot mixture to thicken the liquid. Remove from the heat and stir in the rum.

Chill the mixture in the fridge until cold and churn.

Transfer the ice cream to a shallow freezer-safe container and freeze for at least 3 hours or overnight.

COCONUT MILK ICE CREAM

Rum & Raisin

Yields approx 2 pints / 1 quart

This is one of the first coconut milk ice creams I made and it was love at first taste. It's no surprise that rum is perfect partners with coconut milk.

720ml / 3 cups coconut milk
2 tbsp arrowroot powder
120ml / ½ cup maple syrup
115g / ¾ cup raisins
1 tsp vanilla extract
120ml / ½ cup rum

Mix 60ml / ¼ cup coconut milk with the arrowroot powder in a small bowl and set aside. Put the raisins in a small bowl with 3 tbsp of the rum to soak whilst you make the ice cream.

Pour the rest of the coconut milk into a large saucepan with the maple syrup and bring to a boil. As soon as the mixture begins to boil, stir in the arrowroot mixture to thicken the liquid. Remove from the heat and stir in the vanilla and the rest of the rum.

Chill the mixture in the fridge until cold and churn. During the last few minutes of churning, add the raisins.

Transfer the ice cream to a freezer-safe container and freeze for at least 3 hours or overnight.

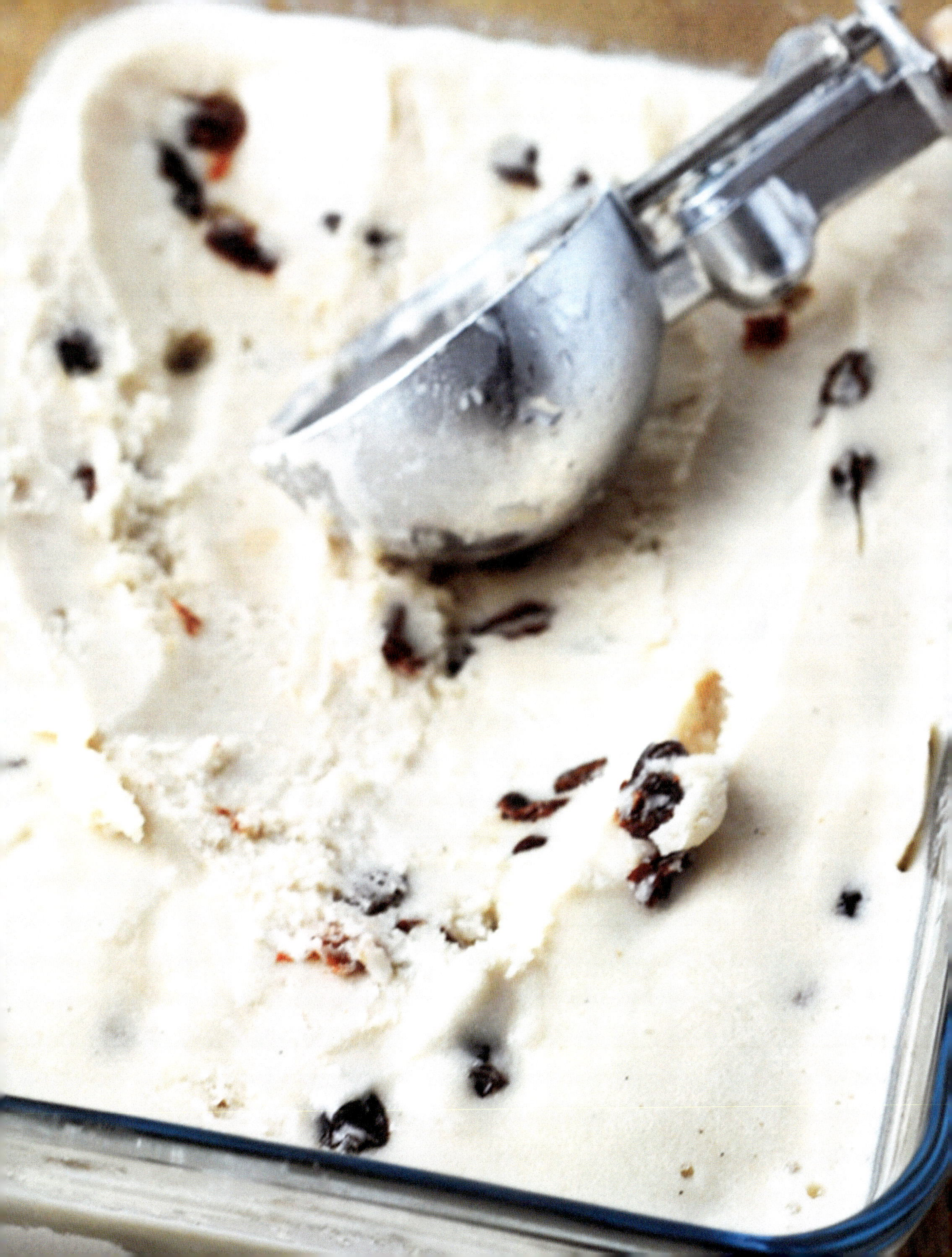

Apple Cider

Yields approx 2 pints / 1 quart

A very refreshing dessert, perfect for a summer's evening. You can even make it into an Apple Cider Float by adding ½ cup of the ice cream to a glass and fill up with 1 cup of apple cider. Add a little cinnamon for an autumn "mulled cider" variation.

720ml / 3 cups coconut milk
2 tbsp arrowroot powder
120ml / ½ cup maple syrup
1 tsp vanilla extract
240ml / 1 cup sweet apple cider

Mix 60ml / ¼ cup coconut milk with the arrowroot powder in a small bowl and set aside.

Pour the rest of the coconut milk into a large saucepan with the maple syrup and cinnamon and bring to a boil. As soon as the mixture begins to boil, stir in the arrowroot mixture to thicken the liquid. Remove from the heat and stir in the vanilla and cider.

Chill the mixture in the fridge until cold and churn.

Transfer the ice cream to a freezer-safe container and freeze for at least 3 hours or overnight.

COCONUT MILK ICE CREAM

Irish Cream

Yields approx 2 pints / 1 quart

If you're a Baileys fan, this is a must-try. Whiskey and non-whiskey drinkers alike will enjoy the rich, creamy and boozy flavours of this ice cream.

720ml / 3 cups coconut milk
2 tbsp arrowroot powder
80ml / ⅓ cup maple syrup
1 heaped tbsp coconut sugar
1 tsp instant coffee
2 tsp cocoa powder
1 tsp vanilla extract
120ml / ½ cup Irish whiskey

Mix 60ml / ¼ cup coconut milk with the arrowroot powder in a small bowl and set aside.

Pour the rest of the coconut milk into a large saucepan with the maple syrup, coconut sugar, coffee and cocoa powder and bring to a boil. As soon as the mixture begins to boil, stir in the arrowroot mixture to thicken the liquid. Remove from the heat and stir in the vanilla and whiskey.

Chill the mixture in the fridge until cold and churn.

Transfer the ice cream to a freezer-safe container and freeze for at least 3 hours or overnight.

Roasted Cherry & Whiskey

Yields approx 2 pints / 1 quart

The combination of roasted cherries, whiskey and chocolate make this a very dark and indulgent dessert. I love the bursts or cherries scattered throughout.

340g / 12oz cherries
1 tbsp coconut sugar
80ml / ⅓ cup whiskey
720ml / 3 cups coconut milk
2 tbsp arrowroot powder
120ml / ½ cup maple syrup
1 tsp vanilla extract
90g / ½ cup chocolate chips

Heat the oven to 200°C / 390°F and roast the cherries with the coconut sugar and 2 tbsp of the whiskey for about 15-20 minutes until they start to shrivel and release their juices.

Meanwhile, take ¼ cup of the coconut milk and mix it with the arrowroot powder in a small bowl. Set aside.

Pour the rest of the coconut milk into a saucepan and with the maple syrup and bring to a boil. As soon as it reaches boiling point, add the arrowroot mixture and stir to thicken. Remove from the heat and stir in the vanilla extract and the rest of the whiskey.

Once the cherries are cooked and cooled, remove their stalks and stones and chop into quarters.

Chill the mixture in the fridge until cold and churn. During the last minute of churning, add in the chopped cherries and chocolate chips.

Transfer the ice cream to a freezer-safe container and freeze for at least 3 hours or overnight.

COCONUT MILK ICE CREAM

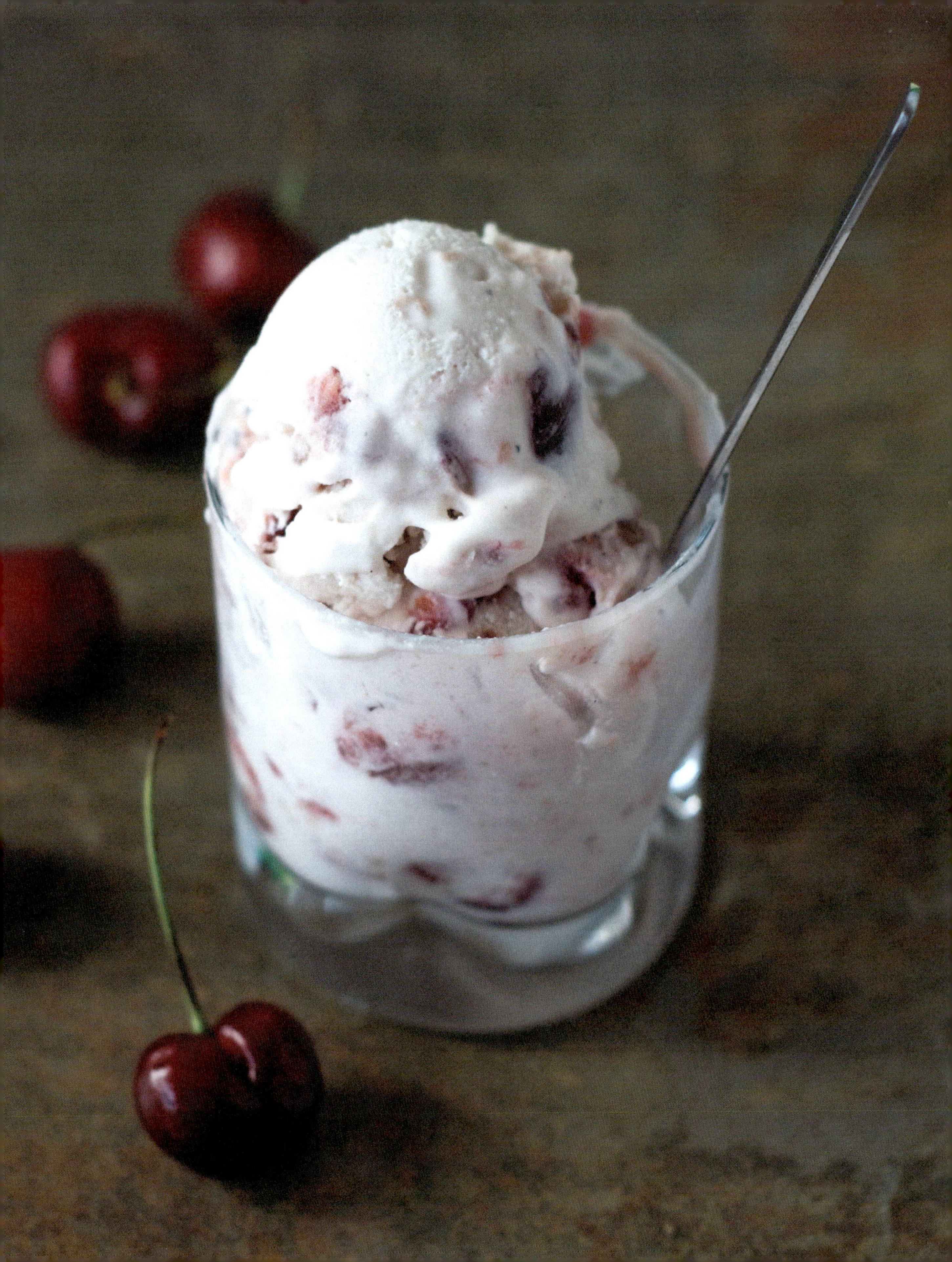

Mojito

Yields approx 2 pints / 1 quart

A fresh and punchy ice cream based on a classic cocktail, the Mojito.

720ml / 3 cups coconut milk
2 tbsp arrowroot powder
120ml / ½ cup maple syrup
Zest and juice from 2 limes
25g / ½ cup fresh mint leaves
60ml / ¼ cup rum

Mix 60ml / ¼ cup coconut milk with the arrowroot powder in a small bowl and set aside.

In a blender, mix the rest of the coconut milk, maple syrup, lime juice and zest and mint leaves together until it forms a smooth mixture.

Pour the mixture into a large saucepan and bring to a boil. As soon as the mixture begins to boil, stir in the arrowroot mixture to thicken the liquid. Remove from the heat and stir in the rum.

Chill the mixture in the fridge until cold and churn.

Transfer the ice cream to a shallow freezer-safe container and freeze for at least 3 hours or overnight.

White Wine

Yields approx 2 pints / 1 quart

A very grown-up and sophisticated ice cream, wonderful served with fresh berries and raspberry coulis (see page 145)

720ml / 3 cups coconut milk
2 tbsp arrowroot powder
120ml / ½ cup maple syrup
240ml / 1 cup sweet white wine

Mix 60ml / ¼ cup coconut milk with the arrowroot powder in a small bowl and set aside.

Pour the rest of the coconut milk into a large saucepan with the maple syrup and bring to a boil. As soon as the mixture begins to boil, stir in the arrowroot mixture to thicken the liquid. Remove from the heat and stir in the white wine.

Chill the mixture in the fridge until cold and churn.

Transfer the ice cream to a freezer-safe container and freeze for at least 3 hours or overnight.

COCONUT MILK ICE CREAM

FLORAL FLAVOURS

Blueberry & Lavender........................95
Chamomile & Vanilla........................96
Elderflower & Lemon........................98
Orange Blossom................................99
Rose Raspberry Ripple......................100

Blueberry & Lavender

Yields approx 2 pints / 1 quart

A fresh and floral ice cream in a beautiful shade of purple.

720ml / 3 cups coconut milk
2 tbsp arrowroot powder
2 tbsp culinary lavender buds
+ extra for serving
200g / 1 cup blueberries
120ml / ½ cup maple syrup
1 tsp vanilla extract
(optional) 1 tbsp alcohol

Mix 60ml / ¼ cup coconut milk with the arrowroot powder in a small bowl and set aside.

Pour the rest of the coconut milk into a large saucepan and bring to a boil. Remove from the heat, add the lavender buds and leave the milk to steep for at least 30 minutes.

Sieve the mixture to remove the lavender buds and pour into a blender, adding the blueberries and maple syrup. Blend until completely smooth then pour into a large saucepan.

Bring the mixture to a boil and as soon as the mixture begins to boil, stir in the arrowroot mixture to thicken the liquid. Remove from the heat and stir in the vanilla and alcohol.

Chill the mixture in the fridge until cold and churn.

Transfer the ice cream to a freezer-safe container and freeze for at least 3 hours or overnight.

Serve with a few buds of dried lavender.

COCONUT MILK ICE CREAM

Chamomile & Vanilla

Yields approx 2 pints / 1 quart

Both chamomile and vanilla are known for their calming properties, so consider this a de-stressing tonic, in the form of a delicious ice cream.

720ml / 3 cups coconut milk
2 tbsp arrowroot powder
120ml / ½ cup maple syrup
3 - 4 tbsp chamomile flowers
1 tbsp vanilla paste
(optional) 1 tbsp alcohol

Mix 60ml / ¼ cup coconut milk with the arrowroot powder in a small bowl and set aside.

Pour the rest of the coconut milk into a large saucepan and bring to a boil. Remove from the heat, add the chamomile flowers and leave the milk to infuse for at least 30 minutes

Sieve the mixture to remove the flowers. Add the maple syrup, stir and bring the mixture to a boil again. As soon as the mixture begins to boil, stir in the arrowroot mixture to thicken the liquid. Remove from the heat and stir in the vanilla and alcohol.

Chill the mixture in the fridge until cold and churn.

Transfer the ice cream to a freezer-safe container and freeze for at least 3 hours or overnight.

COCONUT MILK ICE CREAM

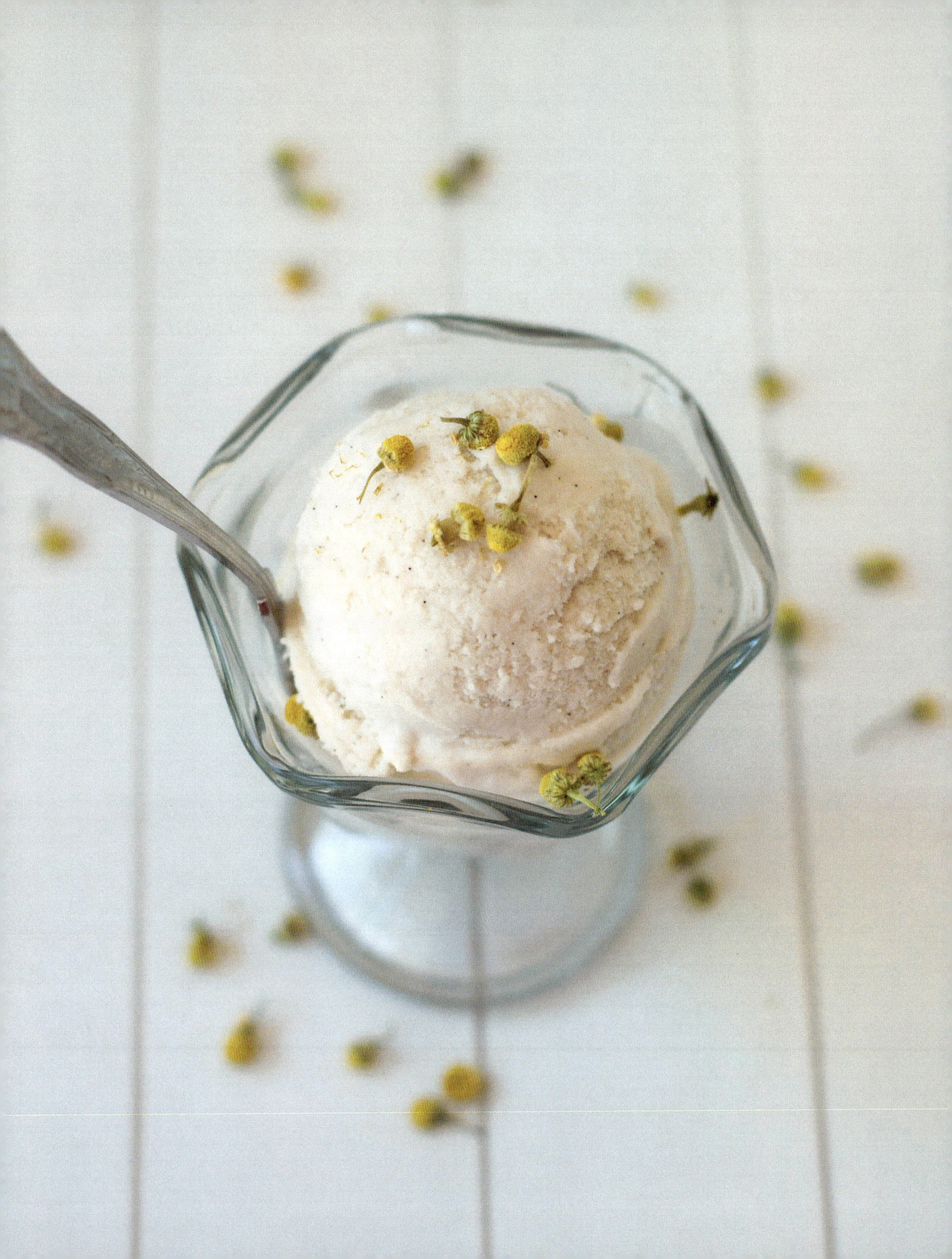

Elderflower & Lemon

Yields approx 2 pints / 1 quart

Tart and zesty lemon paired with delicate and floral elderflower makes one of my all-time favourite flavour combinations. This is a refreshing yet calming ice cream, perfect for spring and summer.

720ml / 3 cups coconut milk
2 tbsp arrowroot powder
120ml / ½ cup maple syrup
80ml / ⅓ cup elderflower cordial
2 tbsp lemon zest
1 tsp vanilla extract
(optional) 1 tbsp alcohol

Mix 60ml / ¼ cup coconut milk with the arrowroot powder in a small bowl and set aside.

Stir the rest of the coconut milk in a large saucepan with the maple syrup, elderflower cordial and lemon zest and bring to a boil. As soon as the mixture begins to boil, stir in the arrowroot mixture to thicken the liquid. Remove from the heat and stir in the vanilla and alcohol.

Chill the mixture in the fridge until cold and churn.

Transfer the ice cream to a freezer-safe container and freeze for at least 3 hours or overnight.

Orange Blossom

Yields approx 2 pints / 1 quart

The musky, citrus and floral aromas of orange blossom water ice cream, served with chopped pistachios is simply heavenly and really captures the flavours of the Middle East.

720ml / 3 cups coconut milk
2 tbsp arrowroot powder
120ml / ½ cup maple syrup
1 tsp vanilla extract
3-4 tbsp orange blossom water
(optional) 1 tbsp alcohol

To serve:
Chopped pistachios

Mix 60ml / ¼ cup coconut milk with the arrowroot powder in a small bowl and set aside.

Stir the rest of the coconut milk in a large saucepan with the maple syrup and bring to a boil. As soon as the mixture begins to boil, stir in the arrowroot mixture to thicken the liquid. Remove from the heat and stir in the vanilla, orange blossom and alcohol.

Chill the mixture in the fridge until cold and churn.

Transfer the ice cream to a shallow freezer-safe container and freeze for at least 3 hours or overnight. Serve with chopped pistachios on top.

COCONUT MILK ICE CREAM

Rose Raspberry Ripple

Yields approx 2 pints / 1 quart

Rose water is an ingredient you don't need a lot of to make an impact. This raspberry ripple ice cream is instantly transformed by just 1 teaspoon of rose water, giving it a wonderfully delicate flavour.

---

1 tsp rose water
1 batch of the Raspberry Coulis (see page 145)
720ml / 3 cups coconut milk
2 tbsp arrowroot powder
120ml / ½ cup maple syrup
1 tsp vanilla extract
(optional) 1 tbsp alcohol

Stir 1 tsp of rosewater into the raspberry coulis and then leave to chill in the fridge until later.

Mix 60ml / ¼ cup coconut milk with the arrowroot powder in a small bowl and set aside to thicken.

Pour the rest of the milk into a saucepan with the maple syrup and bring to a boil, immediately stir in the arrowroot mixture to thicken the liquid. Remove from the heat and stir in the vanilla and alcohol.

Chill in the fridge until cold, then churn.

Transfer the mixture to a freezer-safe container. Pour the coulis over the ice cream and use a skewer to swirl it through.

Freeze for at least 3 hours or overnight.

COCONUT MILK ICE CREAM

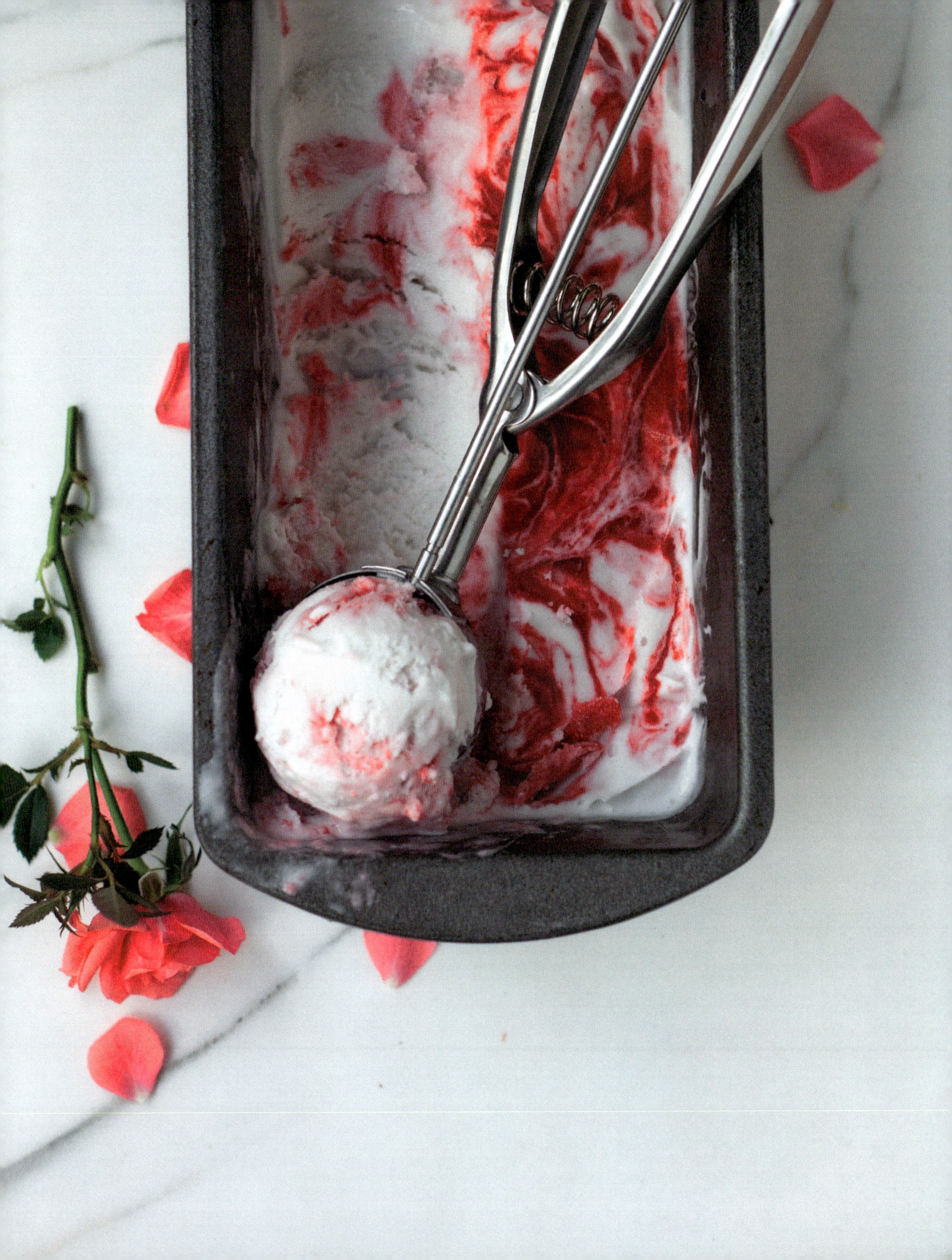

HERBAL & TEA FLAVOURS

Chai Tea..103
Lemon Green Tea.............................104
Fresh Basil & Mint............................106
Malted Maca Chocolate....................107
Earl Grey..108

Chai Tea

Yields approx 2 pints / 1 quart

Enjoy the flavours of this warming tea in the form of a refreshing ice cream. It makes a very comforting afternoon treat.

720ml / 3 cups coconut milk
2 tbsp arrowroot powder
4 Chai tea bags
120ml / ½ cup maple syrup
1 tsp vanilla extract
(optional) 1 tbsp alcohol

Mix 60ml / ¼ cup coconut milk with the arrowroot powder in a small bowl and set aside.

Pour the rest of the coconut milk into a large saucepan and bring to a boil. Remove from the heat, add the tea bags and leave the milk to infuse for at least an hour.

Remove the tea bags. Add the maple syrup, stir and bring the mixture to a boil again. As soon as the mixture begins to boil, stir in the arrowroot mixture to thicken the liquid. Remove from the heat and stir in the vanilla and alcohol.

Chill the mixture in the fridge until cold and churn.

Transfer the ice cream to a freezer-safe container and freeze for at least 3 hours or overnight.

Lemon Green Tea

Yields approx 2 pints / 1 quart

I'll admit that the thing that first attracted me to making this ice cream was the colour. But there is definitely more to it than that... Just 1 tbsp of matcha powder provides the health benefits of 10 servings of Green Tea and it tastes wonderful too!

360ml / 1 ½ cups coconut milk
1 tbsp arrowroot powder
1 tbsp matcha green tea powder
Juice of 1 lemon
60ml / ¼ cup maple syrup
(optional) 1 tbsp alcohol

Mix 60ml / ¼ cup coconut milk with the arrowroot powder in a small bowl and set aside.

Pour the rest of the coconut milk in a saucepan along with the green tea powder, lemon juice and maple syrup. Bring to a boil and whisk for a few minutes until the matcha green tea has been dissolved. Add the arrowroot mixture and lower the heat, whisk for a further couple of minutes until the liquid thickens.

Remove from the heat and stir in the vanilla and alcohol.

Chill in the fridge until cold, then churn. Transfer the mixture to a freezer-safe container and freeze for at least 3 hours or overnight.

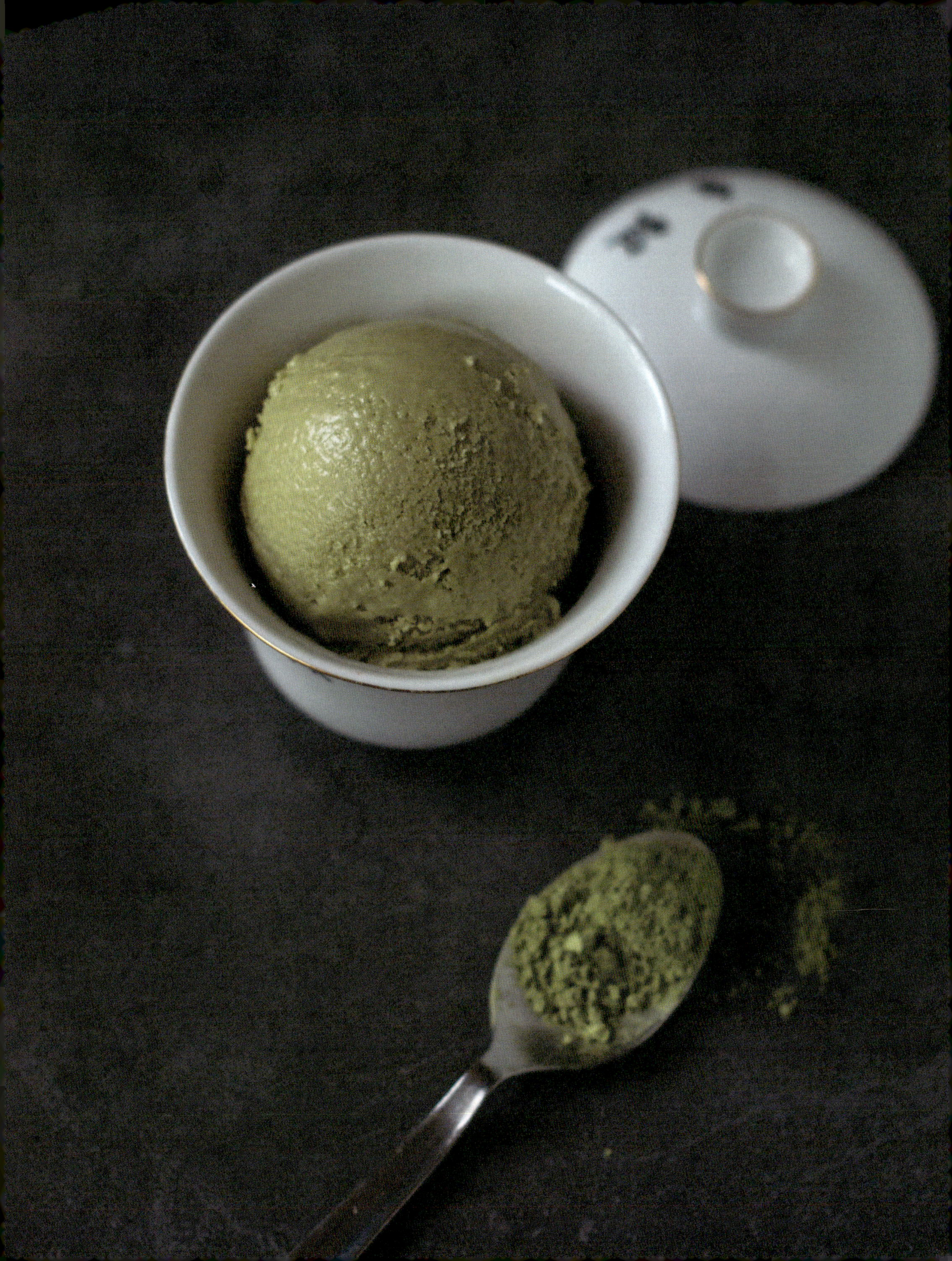

Fresh Basil & Mint

Yields approx 2 pints / 1 quart

Make the most of the herbs in your garden, with this fresh, herby ice cream - it tastes like Summer!

720ml / 3 cups coconut milk
2 tbsp arrowroot powder
50g / 1 cup fresh basil leaves
25g / ½ cup fresh mint leaves
120ml / ½ cup maple syrup
1 tsp vanilla extract
(optional) 1 tbsp alcohol

Mix 60ml / ¼ cup coconut milk with the arrowroot powder in a small bowl and set aside.

Blanch the basil and mint leaves in boiling water for just a few seconds and then transfer into ice cold water to stop them from cooking any further.

Add the herbs with the rest of the coconut milk and the maple syrup in a blender and mix until smooth. Pour the mixture into a large saucepan and bring to a boil.

As soon as the mixture begins to boil, stir in the arrowroot mixture to thicken the liquid. Remove from the heat and stir in the vanilla and alcohol.

Chill the mixture in the fridge until cold and churn.

Transfer the ice cream to a freezer-safe container and freeze for at least 3 hours or overnight.

Malted Maca Chocolate

Yields approx 2 pints / 1 quart

For those of you who love that malted taste, try maca. Not only does it add a delicious malty taste to your dish but it's a superfood too.

720ml / 3 cups coconut milk
2 tbsp arrowroot powder
20g / ¼ cup cocoa powder
2 tbsp maca powder
120ml / ½ cup maple syrup
1 tsp vanilla extract
90g / ½ cup dark chocolate chips
(optional) 1 tbsp alcohol

Mix 60ml / ¼ cup coconut milk with the arrowroot powder in a small bowl and set aside.

Pour the rest of the coconut milk into a large saucepan with the cocoa powder, maca powder and maple syrup and bring to a boil, stirring all the time. As soon as the mixture begins to boil, stir in the arrowroot mixture to thicken the liquid. Remove from the heat and stir in the vanilla, chocolate chips and alcohol. Keep stirring until all the chocolate is melted.

Chill the mixture in the fridge until cold and churn.

Transfer the ice cream to a freezer-safe container and freeze for at least 3 hours or overnight.

Earl Grey

Yields approx 2 pints / 1 quart

Whilst I'm not a big tea drinker, I love the tea flavour in this ice cream. It makes such a refreshing and sophisticated treat. If the weather is too hot to serve tea, serve this instead!

720ml / 3 cups coconut milk
2 tbsp arrowroot powder
4 Earl Grey tea bags
120ml / ½ cup maple syrup
1 tsp vanilla extract
(optional) 1 tbsp alcohol

Mix 60ml / ¼ cup coconut milk with the arrowroot powder in a small bowl and set aside.

Pour the rest of the coconut milk into a large saucepan and bring to a boil. Remove from the heat, add the tea bags and leave the milk to infuse for at least 30 minutes.

Remove the tea bags. Add the maple syrup, stir and bring the mixture to a boil again. As soon as the mixture begins to boil, stir in the arrowroot mixture to thicken the liquid. Remove from the heat and stir in the vanilla and alcohol.

Chill the mixture in the fridge until cold and churn.

Transfer the ice cream to a freezer-safe container and freeze for at least 3 hours or overnight.

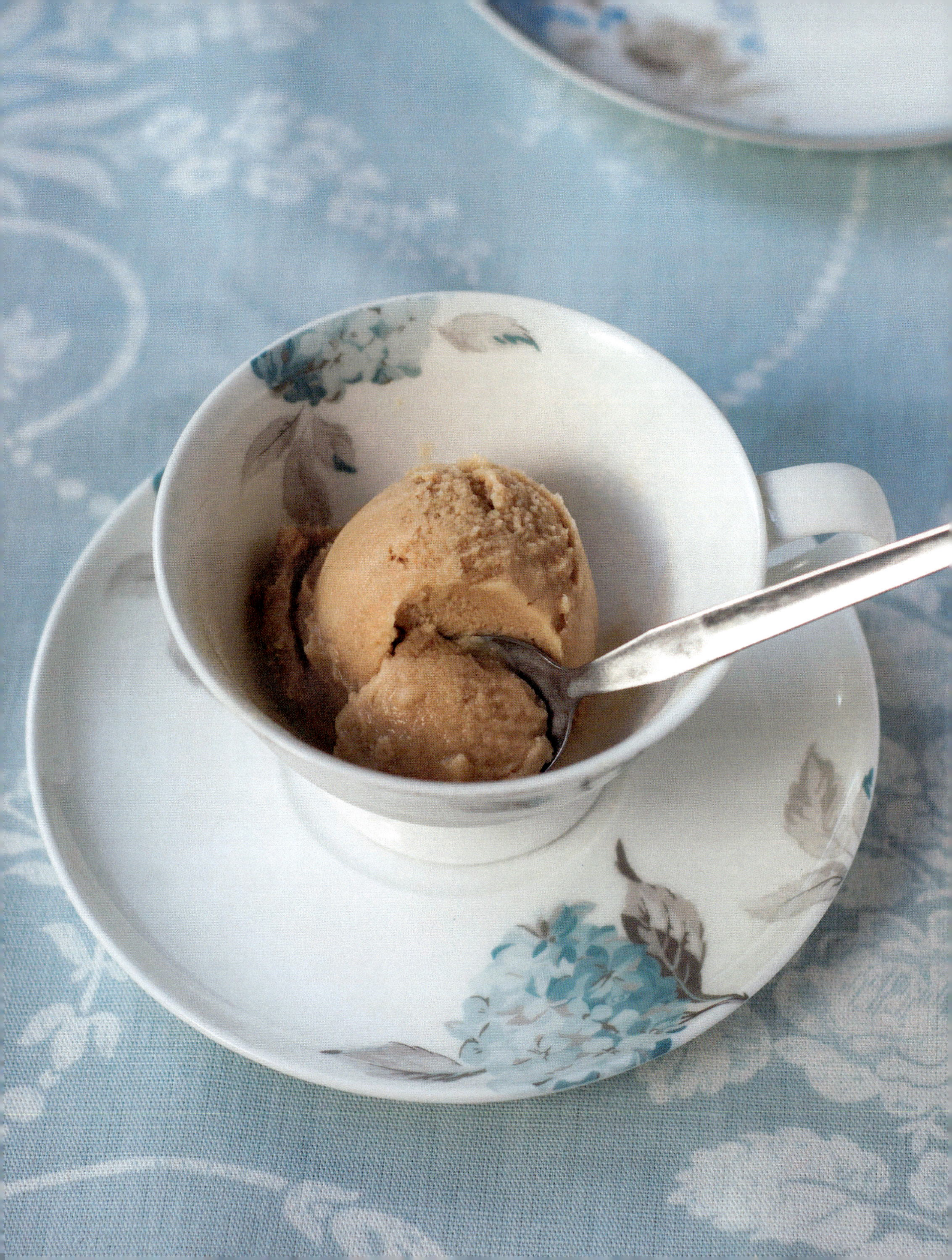

FROZEN DESSERTS & TREATS

COCONUT MILK ICE CREAM

Hot Chocolate Fudge Sundae..112
Black Forest Sundae...114
Coconut Granita...115
Neapolitan Ice Cream Cake...116
Brownie Sandwiches..118
Chocolate Chip Cookie Sandwiches..........................120
Peanut Butter & Chocolate Sandwiches......................121
Chocolate & Vanilla Bars..122
Chocolate-Covered Strawberry & Cream Pops............124
Smashed Blueberry Pops..126
Mango Creamsicles...127
Orange Creamsicles..128
Strawberry Milkshake..130
Chocolate Milkshake..132
Banana Milkshake...133
Emerald Mint Milkshake..134

Hot Chocolate Fudge Sundae

Serves 4

If it were my task to convert someone to coconut milk ice creams, I would simply serve them this Hot Chocolate Fudge Sundae. Creamy vanilla ice cream, with chocolate fudge sauce, topped with coconut whipped cream and chopped roasted peanuts. Heaven.

---

1 batch of vanilla ice cream (see page 26)
1 batch of Hot Chocolate Fudge Sauce (see page 144)

To serve:
Whipped cream (see page 148)
Chopped roasted peanuts

Assemble the sundaes by adding a few scoops of vanilla ice cream to 4 sundae dishes, followed by a generous drizzling of the Hot Chocolate Fudge Sauce, top with the whipped cream and sprinkle some chopped roasted peanuts on top.

Serve immediately!

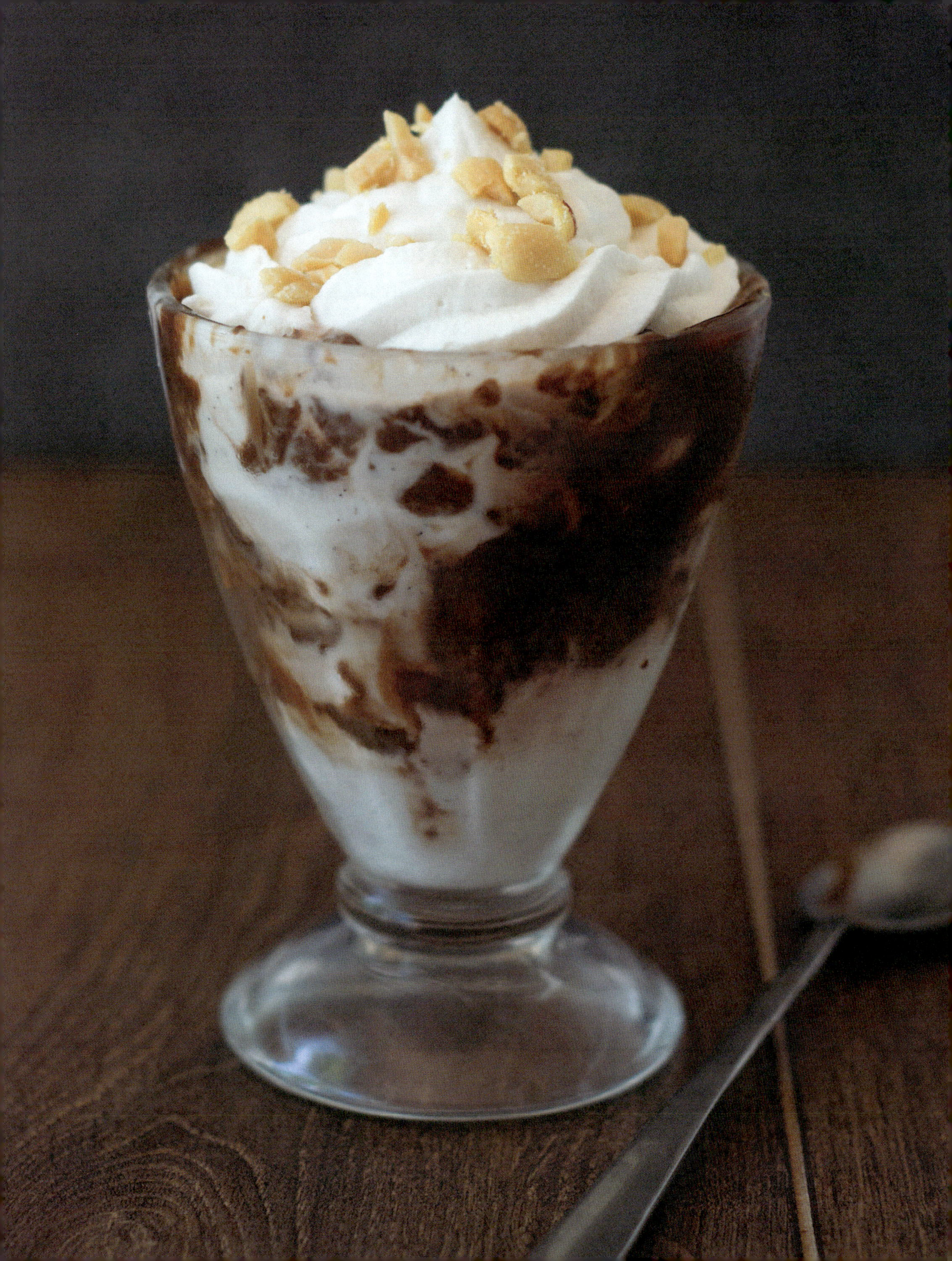

Black Forest Sundae

Serves 4

This sundae is based on the classic seventies dessert - the Black Forest gâteau and uses a mixture of chocolate ice cream, chocolate brownies, brandied cherries and whipped cream to create a devilish dessert.

To assemble:
1 batch of chocolate ice cream (see page 27)
2 chocolate brownies (see page 118)
Brandied cherries (see page 150)

To serve:
4 tbsp whipped cream (see page 148)
1 square of dark chocolate

Assemble the sundaes by crumbling the brownies into the bottom of 4 sundae dishes, followed by a few scoops of chocolate ice cream, a drizzle of the cherries and the syrup, top with whipped cream and grate some dark chocolate on top.

Serve immediately!

Coconut Granita

Serves 4

A cross between a snow cone, slushie and sorbet, granitas are a refreshing treat that are super simple to make, with no special equipment needed! Add in different fruit juices to change the flavour, if you wish.

360ml / 1 ½ cups coconut milk
80ml / ⅓ cup maple syrup
Zest and juice of 1 lime

Place the coconut milk in a saucepan with the maple syrup and the zest and juice from the lime. Heat gently and stir until well combined. Bring to a boil and cook for 3 minutes, then remove from the heat and allow to cool at room temperature.

Pour into a shallow freezer-safe container.

Freeze for 2 hours until it begins to turn a little frosty around the edges. Using a fork, scrape the ice towards the centre and return to the freezer. Keep repeating this process every 30 minutes (approx 4 times) until the mixture is formed of ice crystals.

Serve immediately.

COCONUT MILK ICE CREAM

Neapolitan Ice Cream Cake

Serves 8

How pretty is this ice cream cake? It's quite simple to put together and makes a great dessert for kids. Using an 8.5 x 4.5 inch loaf pan, I used roughly ⅔ of a batch from each ice cream but it's best to see how much you'll need as you go along. Store any leftover ice cream in the freezer!

---

1 batch of strawberry ice cream (see page 48)
1 batch of vanilla ice cream (see page 26)
1 batch of chocolate ice cream (see page 27)

Line a medium-sized loaf pan with parchment paper and scoop in some strawberry ice cream, smoothing it down with the back of a spoon, to create a flat layer, until it comes up ⅓ of the way. Leave to freeze for at least an hour, uncovered.

Repeat with the vanilla ice cream until it comes up ⅔ of the way and freeze again for another hour.

Finally, spoon the chocolate ice cream on top and cover with a piece of parchment paper. Freeze for at least 6 hours or overnight.

To serve, use a warm, sharp knife to cut into slices.

The cake can be kept in the freezer, wrapped in parchment paper, for up to 3 months.

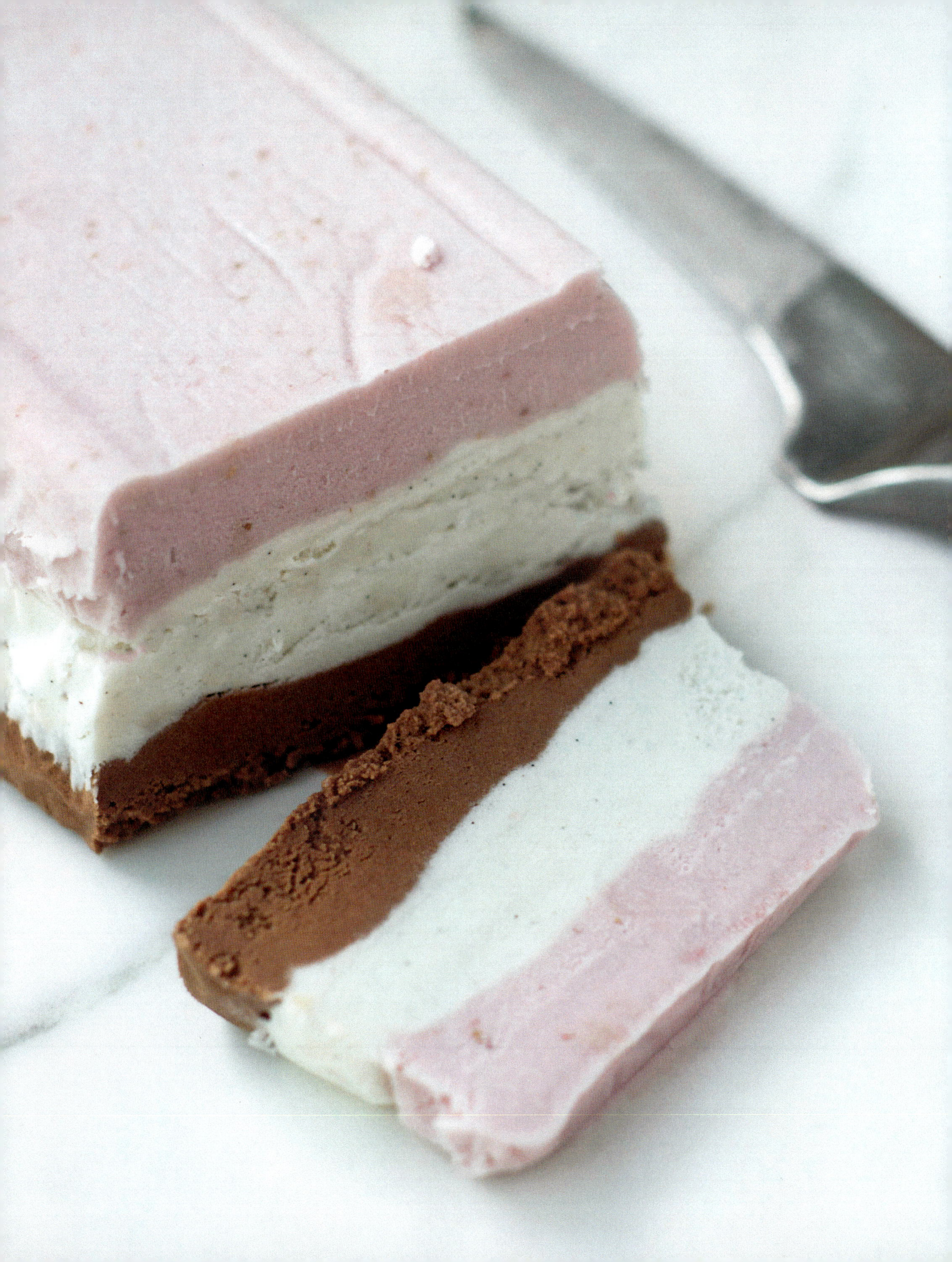

Brownie Sandwiches

Yields 10

These are a little fiddly but *so* worth it! And you can wrap any leftovers and keep in the freezer to enjoy another time.

For the chocolate brownies:
125g / 1 ¼ cups ground almonds
60g / ½ cup cocoa powder
½ tsp baking powder
A pinch of salt
120ml / ½ cup coconut milk
60ml / ¼ cup coconut oil
65g / ¼ cup applesauce
60ml / ¼ cup maple syrup
1 tsp vanilla extract
110g / 4 oz dark chocolate, melted

For the ice cream:
Half a batch of vanilla ice cream on page 26

Preheat the oven to 170°C / 340°F. Line an 8 x 8 brownie tin with parchment paper.

In a large bowl, mix everything together until it forms a thick chocolatey batter. Smooth the batter into the brownie tin and bake for 10-15 minutes until firm but squidgy. Leave to cool completely at room temperature.

Meanwhile, make the vanilla ice cream and after churning, spread the ice cream into another 8 x 8 inch brownie tin lined with 2 layers of parchment paper. Transfer to the freezer and let it freeze completely.

Once the brownies are completely cooled, slice into even-sized squares or slices. Then cut them in half, lengthways to create two brownie halves.

When the ice cream has frozen, remove the ice cream from the tin, lifting out with the sides of the parchment paper and leave to soften until it's easy to slice. Slice into slices or squares the same size as the brownies.

Sandwich the strip of ice cream between two of the brownie halves.

These can be wrapped in parchment paper and kept in the freezer for up to 1 month.

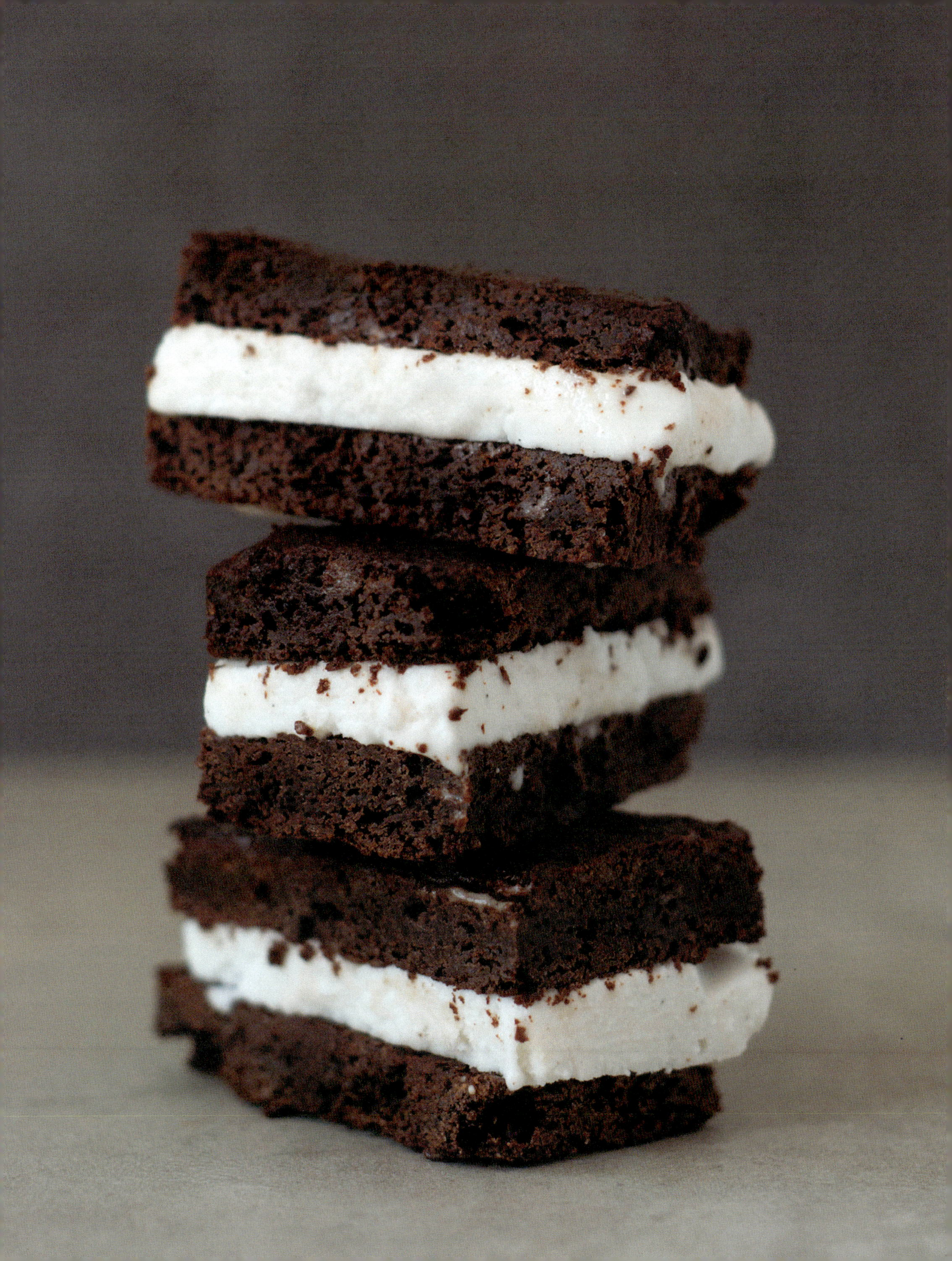

Chocolate Chip Cookie Sandwiches

Yields 12

A classic ice cream sandwich made with secretly healthier ingredients!

For the cookies:
250g / 2 ½ cups ground almonds
½ tsp baking powder
120ml / ½ cup maple syrup
120ml / ½ cup coconut oil, melted
2 tsp vanilla extract
135g / ¾ cup dark chocolate chips

For the ice cream:
Half a batch of vanilla ice cream, (see page 26) softened slightly

Preheat the oven to 170°C / 350°F and line a baking sheet with parchment paper.

In a large bowl, mix the ground almonds, baking powder and salt together. In a separate bowl, whisk the rest of the ingredients together (except the chocolate chips) then add to the bowl of dry ingredients, mixing until well combined.

Fold in the chocolate chips then drop a tbsp of batter onto the baking sheet. Repeat until all the batter is used. You may need to flatten them a little.

Bake for 8-10 minutes until they begin to turn golden brown. Let cool to room temperature before using.

To assemble the cookie sandwiches, place the cookies in the freezer for about 10 minutes to firm them up. Take a scoop of the vanilla ice cream and place it on the bottom of one cookie. Place another on top and gently squish together!

Peanut Butter & Chocolate Sandwiches

Yields 12

Dark chocolate ice cream sandwiched between two rich peanut butter cookies.

For the cookies:
100g / 1 cup ground almonds
½ tsp baking powder
A pinch of salt
125g / ½ cup peanut butter
80ml / ⅓ cup maple syrup
2 tbsp coconut oil
2 tsp vanilla extract

For the ice cream:
Half a batch of chocolate ice cream, (see page 27) softened slightly

Preheat the oven to 170°C / 350°F and line a baking sheet with parchment paper.

With an electric mixer or a food processor, mix all the ingredients together until a smooth dough is formed. Roll into balls then flatten into cookie shapes and place on the baking sheet.

Bake for 7-10 minutes until they begin to turn golden brown. Let cool to room temperature before using.

To assemble the cookie sandwiches, place the cookies in the freezer for about 10 minutes to firm them up. Take a scoop of the chocolate ice cream and place it on the bottom of one cookie. Place another on top and gently squish together!

COCONUT MILK ICE CREAM

Chocolate & Vanilla Bars

Yields 6

These are inspired by Choc Ices or "Klondike Bars" and give that wonderful chocolate crunch shell followed by the creamy vanilla ice cream centre. It's worth noting that these are a *lot* more filling than other choc ices so make in small popsicle molds if serving to kids.

For the ice cream filling:
1 batch of vanilla ice cream (see page 26)

For the chocolate coating:
Magic Shell Chocolate sauce (page 141)

Let the vanilla ice cream soften a little until it's easy enough to spoon into popsicle molds. Fill up 6 popsicle molds and let them freeze completely for at least 5 hours or overnight.

Make the chocolate sauce and let it cool for a few minutes at room temperature.

Take the ice pops out of their molds and dip into the chocolate sauce, making sure both sides are fully coated. It should harden very quickly. Wrap in parchment paper and keep in the freezer.

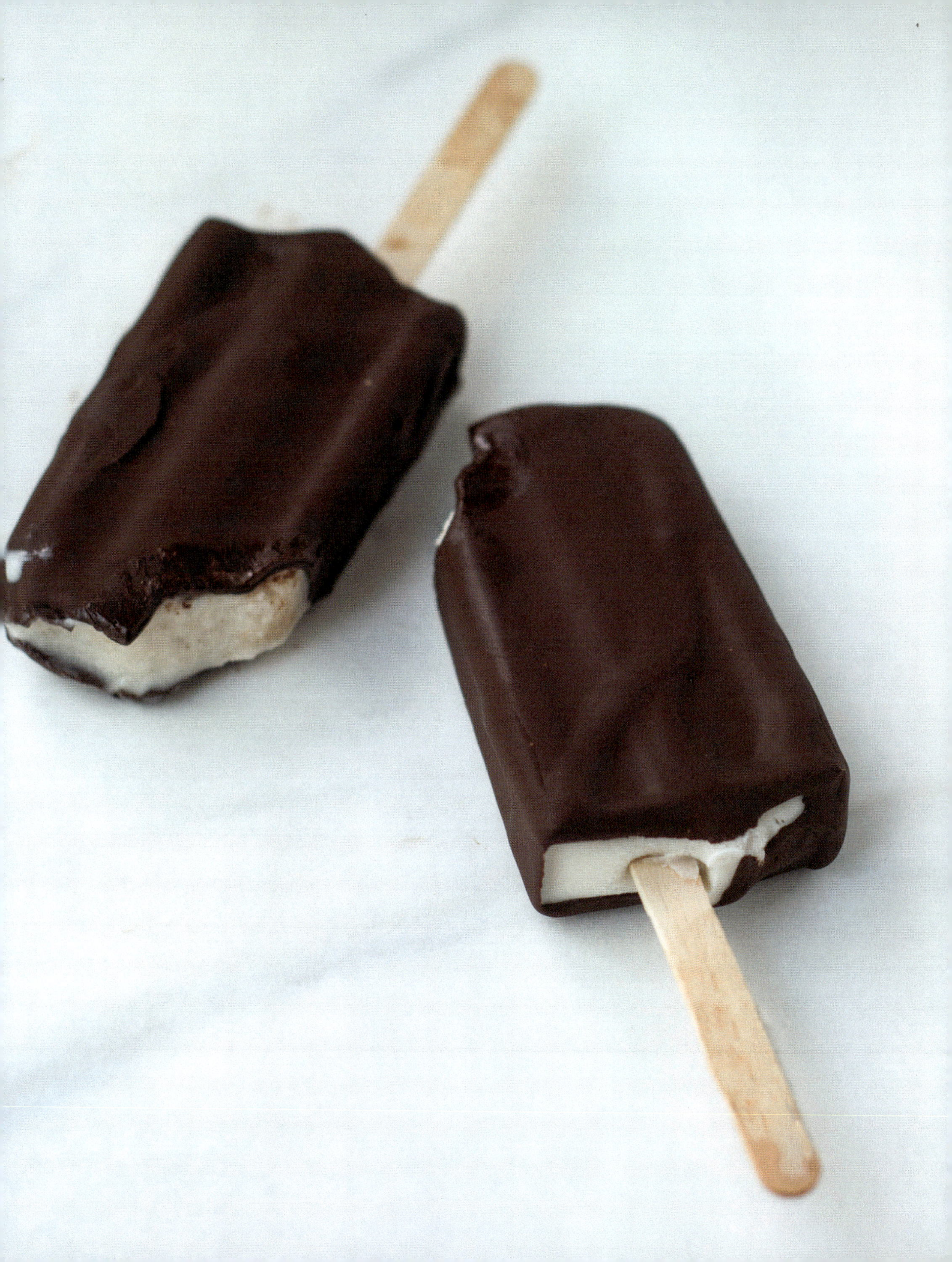

Chocolate-Covered Strawberries & Cream Pops

Yields 6 lollies

These lollies are inspired by a favourite childhood treat we had here in the UK, called "Fab" lollies. I love the way they look and the mixture of flavours and textures they have.

360ml / 1 ½ cups coconut milk
3 tbsp maple syrup
1 tsp vanilla extract
Approx ¾ cup strawberry coulis (see page 145 and use strawberries in place of raspberries)

To serve:
Magic Shell Chocolate sauce (see page 141)
Sprinkles (see page 152)

Mix the coconut milk, maple syrup and vanilla in a blender and blend until smooth. Pour the mixture into popsicle molds ⅔ of the way up. Leave to freeze for about an hour.

Fill the molds the rest of the way up with the strawberry coulis. Add the popsicle sticks in place and freeze for at least 6 hours or overnight.

Once completely frozen, dip the bottom (about ⅓ of the way up) into the Magic Shell Chocolate sauce on page 141 and immediately dip onto a plate full of sprinkles.

Serve immediately or wrap in parchment paper and keep in an air-tight container in the freezer for up to 3 months.

COCONUT MILK ICE CREAM

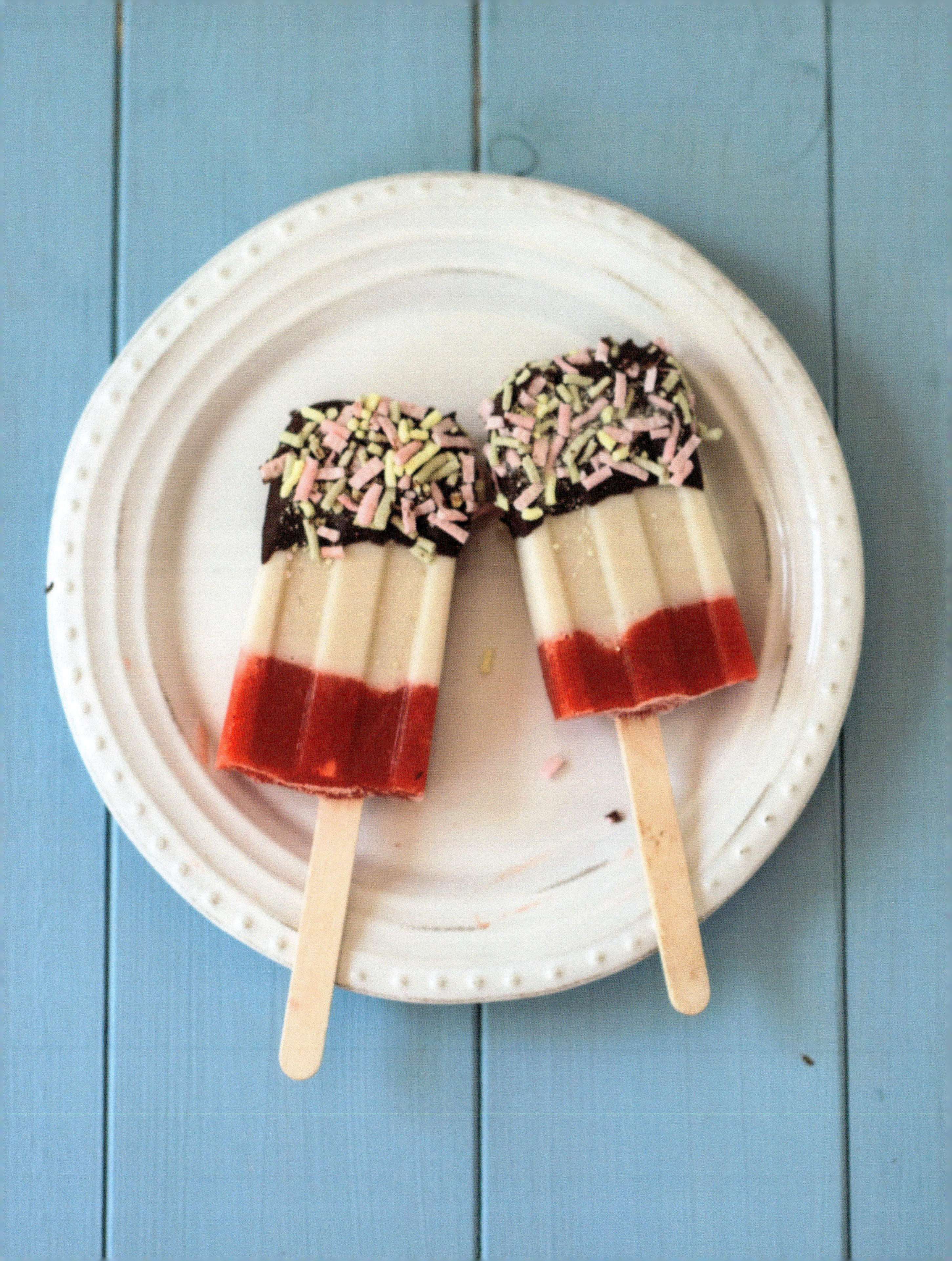

Smashed Blueberry Pops

Yields 6 lollies

The blueberries in these ice lollies retain some of their shape and texture to give small bursts of flavour.

360ml / 1 ½ cups coconut milk
3 tbsp maple syrup
1 tsp vanilla extract
1 cup blueberries

Mix the coconut milk, maple syrup and vanilla in a blender until smooth. Add the blueberries and pulse until they've been "smashed" but not completely blended.

Pour the mixture into popsicle molds and freeze for at least 6 hours or overnight.

Mango Creamsicles

Yields 6 lollies

These creamy, tropical popsicles are the perfect treat for a hot summer's day.

150g / 1 cup frozen mango chunks
120ml / ½ cup coconut milk
3 tbsp maple syrup
1 tsp vanilla extract

Simply mix all the ingredients together in a blender until smooth and frothy and pour into popsicle molds. Freeze for at least 6 hours or overnight.

Orange Creamsicles

Yields 6 lollies

Orange creamsicles are a classic for a reason and this version does not disappoint.

240ml / 1 cup orange juice
120ml / ½ cup coconut milk
3 tbsp maple syrup
1 tsp vanilla extract

Simply mix all the ingredients together in a blender until smooth and frothy and pour into popsicle molds. Freeze for at least 6 hours or overnight.

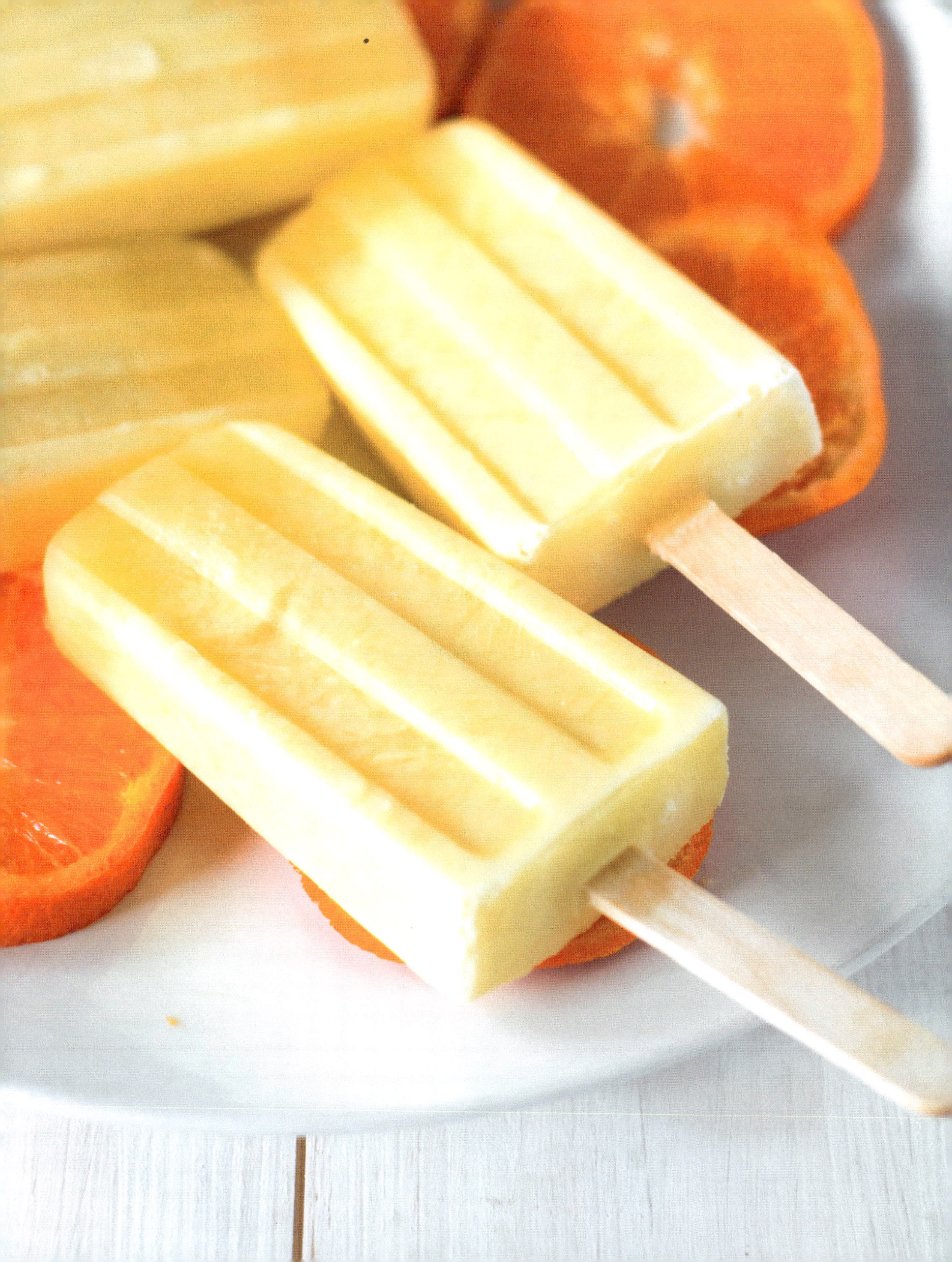

Strawberry Milkshake

Serves 4 - 6

Real strawberry milkshake is one of my favourite drinks. With these milkshakes, you feel like you're drinking something rich and indulgent but the real fruit and healthy ingredients make it almost as virtuous as a smoothie!

1 batch of strawberry ice cream (see page 48)
150g / 1 cup strawberries, hulled and sliced
1 tsp vanilla extract (optional) 1 tsp maca powder*
240ml / 1 cup almond milk

*The maca powder adds a subtle "malted" taste to the milkshake

Scoop the ice cream into a blender with the fresh strawberries, vanilla extract, maca powder (if using) and ½ a cup of the almond milk. Blend until smooth, adding more of the almond milk until you reach a desired consistency.

Pour into milkshake glasses and serve immediately with a straw.

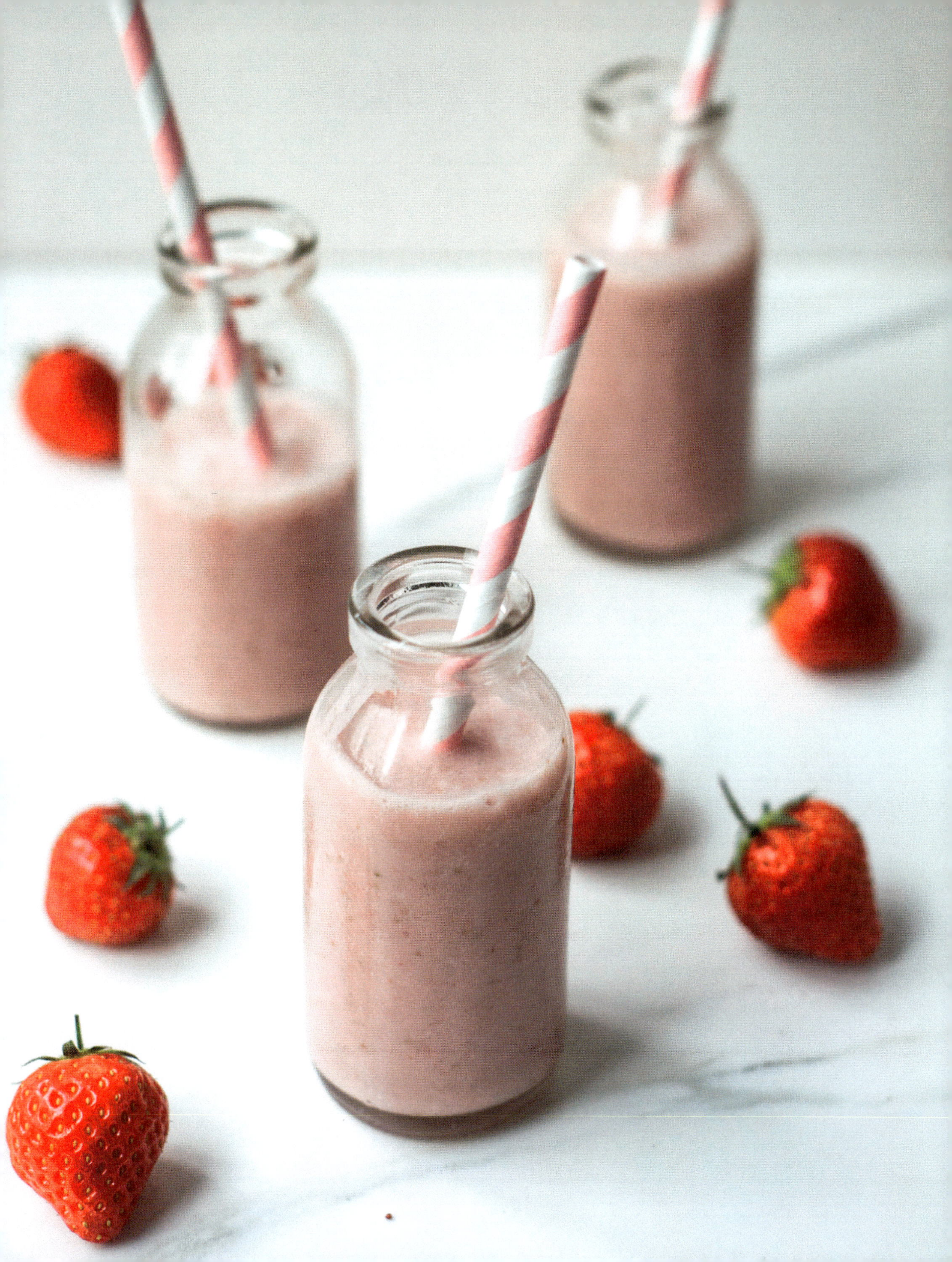

Chocolate Milkshake

Serves 4 - 6

A delicious chocolate beverage transformed into a wonderful dessert by topping with whipped cream and extra chocolate. Mmm!

---

1 batch of chocolate ice cream (see page 27)
1 tsp vanilla extract
(optional) 1 tsp maca powder*
240ml / 1 cup almond milk

To serve:
Whipped cream (see page 148)
Grated dark chocolate

*The maca powder adds a subtle "malted" taste to the milkshake

Scoop the ice cream into a blender with the vanilla extract, maca powder (if using) and ½ a cup of the almond milk. Blend until smooth, adding more of the almond milk until you reach a desired consistency.

Pour into milkshake glasses, top with whipped cream and grated dark chocolate and serve immediately with a straw.

Banana Milkshake

Serves 4 - 6

A creamy milkshake that will satisfy your sweet tooth and give you a healthy boost of energy.

1 batch of vanilla ice cream (see page 26)
4 small *very* ripe bananas, sliced
1 tsp vanilla extract (optional) 1 tsp maca powder*
240ml / 1 cup almond milk

The maca powder adds a subtle "malted" taste to the milkshake

Scoop the ice cream into a blender with the bananas, vanilla extract, maca powder (if using) and ½ a cup of the almond milk. Blend until smooth, adding more of the almond milk until you reach a desired consistency.

Pour into milkshake glasses and serve immediately with a straw.

Emerald Mint Milkshake

Serves 4 - 6

A green, minty milkshake that makes a refreshing treat. Perfect for St. Patrick's Day!

---

1 batch of vanilla ice cream (see page 26)
2 small ripe avocados, peeled and diced
1 tsp peppermint extract
240ml / 1 cup almond milk

To serve:
Whipped cream (see page 148)
Sprinkles (see page 152)

Scoop the ice cream into a blender with the avocados, peppermint extract, and ½ a cup of the almond milk. Blend until smooth, adding more of the almond milk until you reach a desired consistency.

Pour into milkshake glasses, top with whipped cream and sprinkles. Serve immediately with a straw.

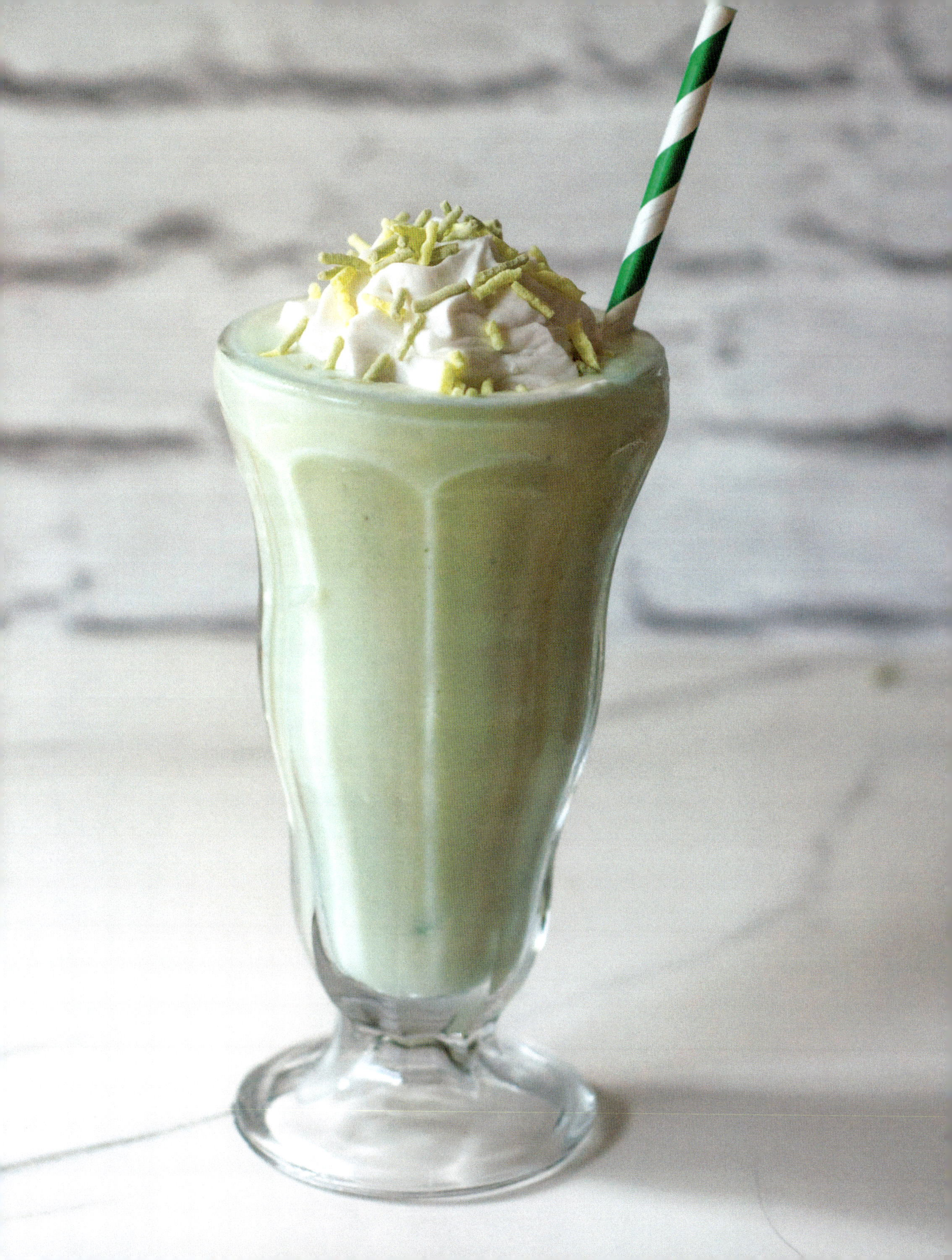

CONES, TOPPINGS & SAUCES

Ice Cream Cones..138
Tuiles & Wafers...140
Magic Shell Chocolate Sauce.......................141
Peanut Butter Sauce...142
Caramel Sauce...143
Hot Chocolate Fudge Sauce........................144
Raspberry Coulis...145
Lemon Curd...146
Whipped Cream...148
Candied Orange Peel.....................................149
Brandied Cherries..150
Caramelized Nuts...151
Sugar-free Sprinkles.......................................152

Ice Cream Cones

Makes 6 - 8 cones

It took a LOT of experimenting but I finally came up with a vegan ice cream cone that is grain-free too! They taste great and hold up very well but are best eaten within a few hours of making as they will start to go soft within a day.

150g / 1 ½ cups ground almonds
2 tbsp arrowroot powder
120ml / ½ cup coconut milk
1 tbsp coconut oil
60ml / ¼ cup maple syrup
1 tsp vanilla extract

Variation: Add 2 tbsp cocoa powder to the mixture and dip the top into some magic shell chocolate (see page 141) to make it into a chocolate cone!

Preheat your waffle cone maker or preheat the oven to 160°C / 320°F if you don't have a waffle cone maker.

Combine all the ingredients together in a food processor and mix until very smooth and thick.

To make with the waffle cone maker, simply drop 1 tablespoon of the batter onto the iron and close the lid. It should take about 2 minutes but use the first cone as your "test" cone to see how long it takes.

To make in the oven, draw a 6 inch circle onto a sheet of paper and place it onto a baking sheet. Place a sheet of greaseproof paper over the top and use the circle underneath as a guide. Drop 1 tbsp of the mixture into the centre of the circle and smooth out as thin as possible using a spatula. Bake for about 10 minutes or until it begins to turn golden brown.

When the waffles are ready, work very quickly to shape them into cones using a waffle cone shaper.

COCONUT MILK ICE CREAM

Made with a waffle cone maker

Baked in an oven

Tuiles & Wafers

Makes 12 - 20

This is the same recipe as the ice cream cones but used in a slightly different way. Wafers and tuiles are a great edition to any sundae!

150g / 1 ½ cups ground almonds
2 tbsp arrowroot powder
120ml / ½ cup coconut milk
1 tbsp coconut oil
60ml / ¼ cup maple syrup
1 tsp vanilla extract

Preheat the oven to 170°C / 350°F and line a baking sheet with parchment paper.

Combine all the ingredients together in a food processor and mix until very smooth and thick.

Dollop a small amount of the batter onto a baking sheet and spread as thinly as possible into the size circle you want. Only bake a few at a time. Bake for 8-10 minutes until golden brown.

Working quickly, as soon as they are removed from the oven, place the tuiles onto a rolling pin and let it take the shape. After about 10 seconds it will have firmed up and you can remove it from the rolling pin.

You can also try using an upside down muffin tin or shot glass, to make edible bowls or roll them into cigar wafers using a wooden spoon handle.

COCONUT MILK ICE CREAM

Magic Shell Chocolate Sauce

Yields approx 180ml / ¾ cup

The "magic" of this sauce is that when it's poured onto a cold surface, it quickly hardens into a firm, crispy shell. It makes a fun and delicious ice cream topping.

250g / 1 cup dark chocolate, broken into small chunks
4 tbsp coconut oil

Gently melt the dark chocolate in a heat-proof bowl over a pot of simmering water and once melted, stir in the coconut oil to make a runny sauce.

Let the sauce cool to room temperature before using.

Peanut Butter Sauce

Yields approx 180ml / ¾ cup

This crunchy peanut butter sauce is amazing poured over ice creams, especially the nutty and chocolate varieties. It's super simple to make too!

120ml / ½ cup maple syrup
65g ¼ cup crunchy peanut butter*

*Use smooth peanut butter, if you prefer

Simply pour the maple syrup and peanut butter into a small saucepan and stir over a medium heat. Keep stirring until creamy and well combined. It should take approximately 1 minute.

Remove from the heat and leave to cool at room temperature before using.

Store in an air-tight container in the fridge for up to 5 days.

COCONUT MILK ICE CREAM

Caramel Sauce

Yields approx 180ml / ¾ cup

This sauce can easily be turned into a salted caramel sauce by simply adding a generous pinch of salt when cooking. Delicious served over almost anything!

120ml / ½ cup evaporated coconut milk (see page 14)
35g / ¼ cup coconut sugar
1 tsp vanilla extract
(optional) Pinch of salt

Pour the coconut milk and coconut sugar into a small saucepan and stir together on a low heat until well combined and thickened. Add the salt if using.

Remove from the heat and stir in the vanilla extract.

Keep in an air-tight container in the fridge for up to 5 days.

Hot Chocolate Fudge Sauce

Yields approx 120ml / ½ cup

Silky, indulgent and very moreish, this Hot Chocolate Fudge Sauce is delicious over most ice creams but is especially wonderful in the Hot Chocolate Fudge Sundae on page 112.

25g / ¼ cup dark chocolate, chopped
80ml / ⅓ cup evaporated coconut milk (see page 14)
1 - 2 tbsp maple syrup
1 tsp vanilla extract
Pinch of salt

Gently melt the chocolate in a heat-proof bowl over a pot of simmering water.

Once melted, stir in the rest of the ingredients until well mixed and you are left with a thick but runny sauce. Adjust sweetness, if desired.

Leave to cool at room temperature before serving with ice cream. It can be kept in an air-tight container in the fridge for up to 5 days.

Raspberry Coulis

Yields approx 80ml / ⅓ cup

A sweet, fruity coulis to add some extra flavour and sweetness to your desserts. Drizzle over your favourite ice creams or add a tablespoon to the bottom of a sundae glass. Feel free to swap the raspberries for other berries or a mixture of berries to make different flavours.

65g / ½ cup raspberries
Juice of 1 lemon
1 tbsp maple syrup

Mix all the ingredients together in a blender or food processor until you have a smooth purée.

Pour the mixture into a small saucepan and simmer for about 5 minutes until thickened and reduced.

Keep in the fridge for up to 3 days.

Lemon Curd

Yields approx 120ml / ½ cup

Lemon curd is one of my most favourite things in life. This version has the same classic flavour with a thick, custard-like texture. Delicious at the bottom of sundaes or dolloped on top of ice creams.

60ml / ¼ cup coconut milk
3 tbsp arrowroot powder
60ml / ¼ cup maple syrup
Zest & juice of 1 large lemon
(optional) ¼ tsp turmeric

Pour the coconut milk into a small saucepan and whisk in the arrowroot powder until dissolved.

Bring the mixture to a boil, stirring all the while and drizzle in the maple syrup. Once the mixture thickens, remove from the heat.

Add lemon zest and juice and mix well to combine. If using, add the turmeric for a colour boost. Allow to cool at room temperature and give a good whisk before using.

Keep in the fridge for up to 3 days.

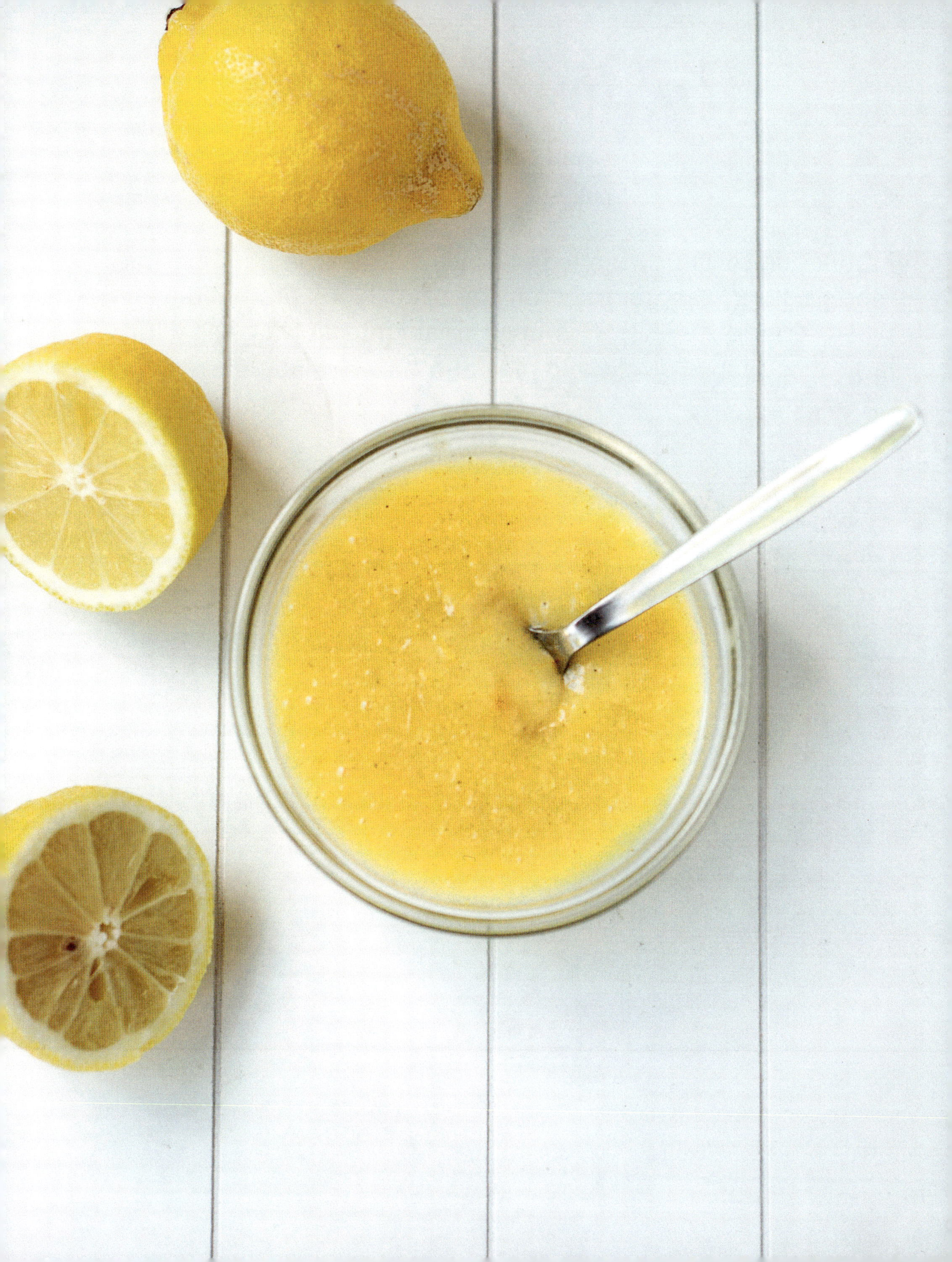

Whipped Cream

Yields approx 120g / ½ cup

I think that coconut whipped cream is the best whipped cream there is. It's so easy to make too! To make it look professional when serving, spoon the whipped cream into an icing bag with a large star-shaped nozzle and pipe into a swirl shape.

120g / ½ cup coconut cream (see page 14)
1 - 2 tbsp maple syrup
1 tsp vanilla extract

For the absolute best results, make sure your bowl and whisk are chilled before starting.

Add the coconut cream to a cold bowl and whisk for a few minutes until thickened. Add the maple syrup and vanilla extract then whisk again.

Once whipped, use immediately or store in the fridge, covered in cling film, for up to 2 weeks.

COCONUT MILK ICE CREAM

Candied Orange Peel

I could eat this all day! Try chilling them in the fridge and dipping them into the Magic Shell Chocolate sauce (see page 141) for an even more delicious treat. This peel makes a great topping for any citrus or chocolate based ice cream.

1 large orange
480ml / 2 cups water
60ml / ¼ maple syrup
½ cup coconut flakes
2 tbsp coconut sugar*

You could use 50g / ¼ cup of xylitol to replace both the coconut flakes and coconut sugar

Remove the peel from the orange by first cutting into quarters, then slicing the pith away from the skin. Try and remove as much of the pith as possible. Once you're left with just the orange peel, slice into long, thin strips.

Add the strips to a saucepan with one cup of the water, bring to a boil and then reduce to a simmer for 30 minutes. Strain and add back to the saucepan with the other half of the water and the maple syrup. Bring to the boil and lower to a simmer for an hour. The liquid will reduce into a lovely syrup which you can save for another recipe!

In a food processor, mix together the coconut flakes and coconut sugar until you have a fine, sugar-like mixture. Sprinkle onto a plate.

Strain the peel and toss about in the mixture until well coated. Leave to dry out on a baking sheet for at least 24 hours. Once dried, store in an airtight container for up to 1 month.

COCONUT MILK ICE CREAM

Brandied Cherries

If you'd rather make your own than buy store-bought brandied or kirsch cherries - this is for you! Feel free to add any spices and flavourings such as cinnamon and vanilla extract. Use the cherries to make the delicious Black Forest Sundae on page 114.

80ml / ⅓ cup maple syrup
120ml / ½ cup water or cherry juice
450g / 1lb sweet cherries, pitted and stemmed
240ml / 1 cup brandy

In a saucepan, pour in the maple syrup and water (or cherry juice) and bring to a boil. Reduce to a simmer and add the cherries. Simmer for a further 5 minutes. Remove from heat, and stir in the brandy.

Let cool slightly before transferring the cherries into clean jars. Fill up the jars with the syrup and refrigerate, uncovered for a couple of hours, then secure with a lid and refrigerate overnight. The longer you leave the cherries the better they will taste! You can keep them in the fridge for up to 3 months.

Caramelized Nuts

Yields approx 150g / 1 cup

It's hard not to eat all of these before the time they make it to the ice cream but if you can restrain yourself, these nuts can be used to make an amazing Pecan Praline ice cream (see page 55) or can simply be used as a topping.

1 tsp coconut oil
150g / 1 cup of mixed nuts or nuts of your choice
2 tbsp maple syrup
1 tbsp coconut sugar
A pinch of salt

Preheat the oven to 170°C / 350°F and lightly grease a baking sheet with the coconut oil. Prepare a separate sheet of tin foil for when they come out of the oven.

In a bowl, mix together the rest of the ingredients with a spoon until well combined. Spread onto the baking sheet and arrange evenly.

Bake for 10-15 minutes until well coated and golden brown. Remove from the oven and tip onto the sheet of tin foil. Be careful as they will be very hot! Leave them to cool for at least 10 minutes.

Once cooled, break up any clusters of nuts. Keep in an air-tight container for up to 3 weeks at room temperature.

COCONUT MILK ICE CREAM

Sugar-free Sprinkles

Yields approx 240g / ½ cup

Sometimes a bowl of ice cream is just not complete without some sprinkles on top and they don't have to be filled with unhealthy ingredients to look good! These sprinkles use all natural colourings and a sugar-free sweetener.

---

1 ¼ cups xylitol* (approx 230g)
35g / ¼ cup arrowroot powder
1 tsp vanilla extract
2-4 tbsp coconut milk

Natural colourings:
Pink - Beet powder
Yellow - Turmeric Powder
Green - Matcha powder
Dark green - Spirulina powder
Blue - Cabbage juice

*You can substitute for other granulated sugar-free sweeteners but use the cup measurement as the weights vary.

Line 2 baking sheets with parchment paper.

Place the xylitol and arrowroot powder in a food processor and grind until a fine powdered sugar is formed. Transfer the powdered sugar to a large bowl and add the vanilla extract. Stir in 1 tbsp of coconut milk at a time until you achieve a thick but runny icing consistency.

If you wish to use different colourings, separate the mixture into bowls and add a tbsp of colouring and mix well. Pour the contents of one of the bowls into an icing bag with a small writing nozzle and pipe straight lines onto the baking sheets. Make sure they don't touch each other and if the mixture becomes to dry/stiff, simply dip the nozzle into a cup of boiled water and it will loosen up.

Repeat with the other colours, if using. Leave the piped lines to dry out completely for 24 hours. After they've dried out, use a knife to break them up into sprinkles (or you can just break them in your hands.)

Store in an air tight container in the fridge for up to 2 months.

COCONUT MILK ICE CREAM

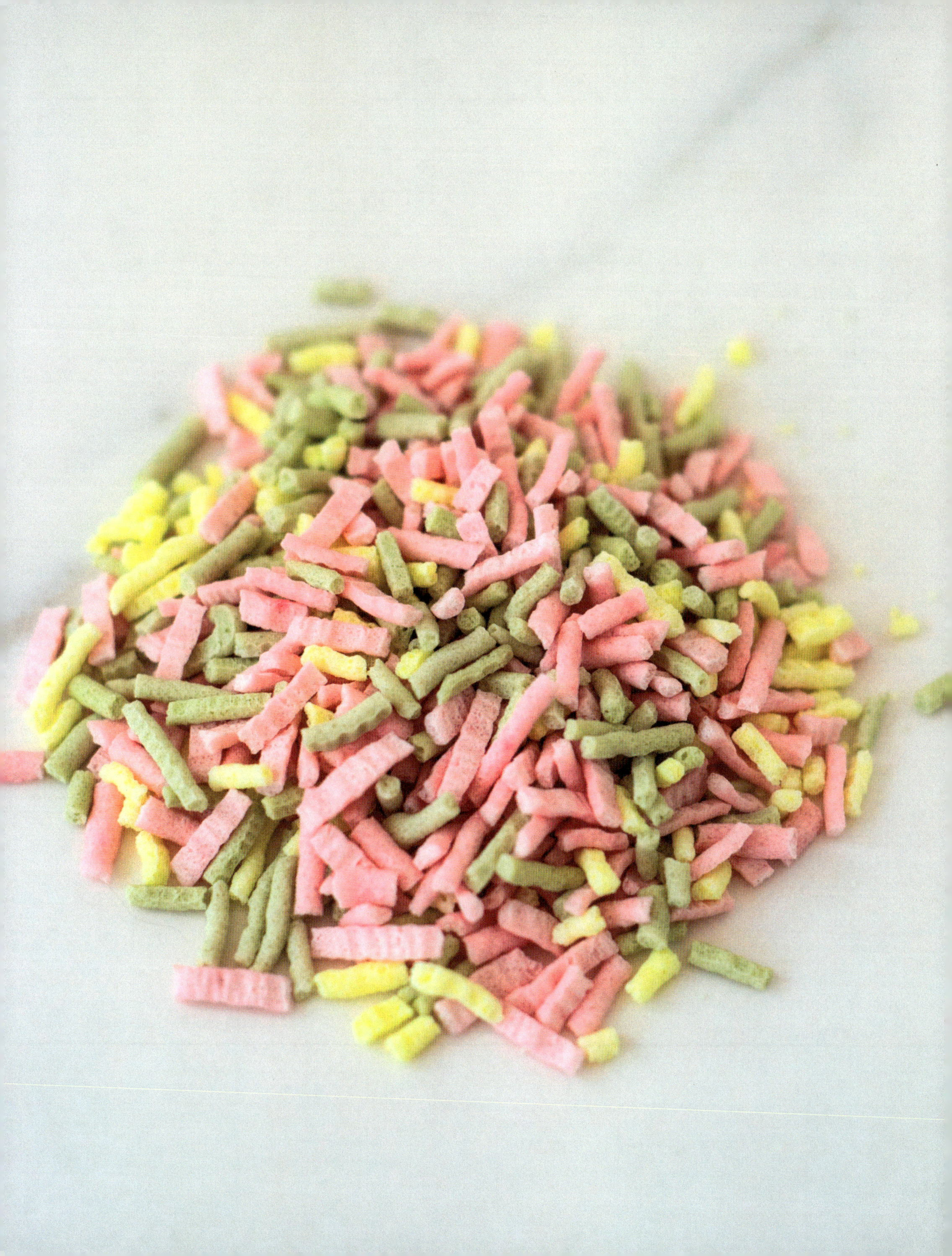

RESOURCES

CHOCOLATE

Willie's Cacao - Dark Chocolate
Vegan, dairy-free, soy-free, gluten-free
willieschocolateshop.com
UK

Tropical Source Semi Sweet Chocolate Chips
Vegan, dairy-free, gluten-free
UK - goodnessdirect.co.uk
USA - sunspire.com

Enjoy Life Semi-Sweet Chocolate Chips & Dark Chocolate
Vegan, dairy-free, soy-free, gluten-free
enjoylifefoods.com
USA, Canada & Australia

COCONUT MILK

Amaizin Organic Rich Coconut Milk
Full fat. Just coconut, water and guar gum
amaizin.com
UK

Thai Kitchen's Organic Coconut Milk
Full fat. Just coconut, water and guar gum
thaikitchen.com
USA & Canada

COCONUT SUGAR

Biona Organic Coconut Palm Sugar
biona.co.uk
UK

Nutiva Organic Coconut Sugar
nutiva.com
USA, Canada, EU, UK & China

ICE CREAM MAKERS

cuisinart.co.uk / cuisinart.com
UK & USA

ICE CREAM SCOOPS

Oxo Trigger Ice Cream Scoop
oxouk.com / oxo.com
UK, USA, EU, India & Asia

COCONUT MILK ICE CREAM

GRAMS TO OUNCES
CONVERSION TABLE

Solid	Liquid
25g = 1 oz	25ml = 1 oz
50g = 2 oz	50ml = 2 oz
75g = 3 oz	75ml = 3 oz
100g = 4 oz	110ml = 4oz
125g = 4.5 oz	125ml = 4.5 oz
150g = 5 oz	150ml = 5 oz
175g = 6 oz	175ml = 6 oz
225g = 8 oz	200ml = 7 oz
250g = 9 oz	225ml = 8 oz
325g = 12 oz	250ml = 8.5 oz
350g = 12.5 oz	275ml = 10 oz
375g = 13 oz	300ml = 10.5 oz
400g = 14 oz	350ml = 12 oz
450g = 1 lb	400ml = 14 oz
700g = 1.5 lbs	450ml = 16 oz
1 kg = 2.5 lbs	575ml = 20 oz

INDEX

A

Almonds
  Almond Milk
in Banana Milkshake 133
in Chocolate Milkshake 132
in Emerald Mint Milkshake 134
in Strawberry Milkshake 130
  Ground Almonds
Chocolate Chip Cookie Sandwiches 120
in Brownie Sandwiches 118
in Christmas Pudding 83
in Ice Cream Cones 138
in Tuiles & Wafers 140
Rhubarb Almond Crumble Ice Cream 75
  Salted Almonds Ice Cream 63
Apples
  Apple Pie Ice Cream 79
Apricots
  Apricot Ice Cream 53
  Dried Apricots
Apricot Ice Cream 53
in Christmas Pudding Ice Cream 83

B

Bananas
  Banana Milkshake 133
  Caramelized Banana Ice Cream 49
Basil
  Fresh Basil Mint Ice Cream 106
Beetroot
  Red Velvet Beetroot Cake Ice Cream 80
Blueberries
  Blueberry & Lavender Ice Cream 95
  Smashed Blueberry Pops 126
Brandy
  Brandied Cherries 150
Brownies
  Brownie Sandwiches 118

C

Cashews
  Caramelized Nuts 151
  Cashew Cookie Dough Chip 28
Cayenne Pepper
  in Mayan Chocolate Ice Cream 68
Chai Tea
  Chai Tea Ice Cream 103
Chamomile
  Chamomile & Vanilla Ice Cream 96
Cherries
  Brandied Cherries 150
  in Black Forest Sundae 114
  Roasted Cherry & Whiskey Ice Cream 90
Chestnut
  Chestnut Caramel Ice Cream 59
Chocolate
  Chocolate Brownie Ice Cream 31
  Chocolate Chip Ice Cream 30
  Chocolate-Covered
  Strawberries & Cream Pops 124
  Chocolate Hazelnut Ice Cream 60
  Chocolate Ice Cream 27
  Chocolate Milkshake 132
  Magic Shell Chocolate Sauce 141
  Chocolate & Vanilla Bars 122
  Hot Chocolate Fudge Sundae 112
  in Black Forest Sundae 114
  in Brownie Sandwiches 118
  in Cashew Cookie Dough Chip Ice Cream 28
  Hot Chocolate Fudge Sauce 144
  in Mint Chocolate Chip Ice Cream 34
  in Mocha Ice Cream 35
  in Neapolitan cake 116
  in Peanut Butter Chocolate Swirl Ice Cream 56
  in Red Velvet Beetroot Cake Ice Cream 80
  Resources 154
Cider
  Apple Cider Ice Cream 88
Cinnamon
  in Apple Pie Ice Cream 79
  in Christmas Pudding Ice Cream 83
  in Mayan Chocolate Ice Cream 68

COCONUT MILK ICE CREAM

Coconut Cream
  How to make coconut cream 14
  Whipped Cream 148
Coconut Milk
  Health Benefits 8
  Homemade Coconut Milk 13
  Resources 154
Coconuts
  Coconut Granita 115
  Coconut Ice Cream 37
Coconut Sugar
  Resources 154
Coffee
  Coffee & Walnut Cake Ice Cream 82
  in Irish Cream Ice Cream 89
  in Mocha Ice Cream 35

D

Dates
  Date Ice Cream 46
  in Christmas Pudding Ice Cream 83

E

Earl Grey Tea
  Earl Grey Ice Cream 108
Elderflower
  Elderflower & Lemon Ice Cream 98

G

Ginger
  Fresh Ginger Ice Cream 67
  in Sweet Curry Ice Cream 72
Green Tea
  Lemon Green Tea Ice Cream 104

H

Hazelnuts
  Chocolate Hazelnut Ice Cream 60

L

Lavender
  Blueberry & Lavender Ice Cream 95
Lemons
  Elderflower & Lemon Ice Cream 98
  Lemon Curd 146
  Lemon Green Tea Ice Cream 104
  Lemon Poppy Seed Muffin Ice Cream 76
Limes
  in Coconut Granita 115
  in Mojito Ice Cream 92
  Papaya & Lime Ice Cream 41

M

Maca
  in Banana Milkshake 133
  in Chocolate Milkshake 132
  in Strawberry Milkshake 130
  Malted Maca Chocolate Ice Cream 107
Mangoes
  Mango Creamsicles 127
  Mango & Passionfruit Ice Cream 38
Melon
  Sweet Melon Ice Cream 45
Mint
  Emerald Mint Milkshake 134
  Fresh Mint & Lime Ice Cream 106
  Mint Chocolate Chip Ice Cream 34

O

Orange
  Orange Ice Cream 52
Orange Blossom
  Orange Blossom Ice Cream 99
Oranges
  Candied Orange Peel 149
  in Chinese Five-Spice Ice Cream 71
  in Christmas Pudding Ice Cream 83
  Orange Blossom Ice Cream 99
  Orange Creamsicles 128
  Orange Ice Cream 52

P

Papayas
  Papaya & Lime Ice Cream 41
Passionfruit
  Mango & Passionfruit Ice Cream 38
Peaches
  Peaches & Cream Ice Cream 50
Peanuts
  Peanut Butter
Peanut Butter & Chocolate Sandwiches 121
Peanut Butter Chocolate Swirl Ice Cream 56
Peanut Butter Sauce 142
Pecans
  Pecan Praline Ice Cream 55
Pineapples
  Roasted Pineapple Ice Cream 40

COCONUT MILK ICE CREAM

Pistachios
   Pistachio Ice Cream 58
Plums
   Roasted Plum & Cardamom Ice Cream 42
Pomegranate
   Pomegranate Ice Cream 44
Pumpkin
   Pumpkin Pie Ice Cream 78

R

Raspberries
   Raspberry Coulis 145
   Rose Raspberry Ripple Ice Cream 100
Rhubarb
   Rhubarb Almond Crumble Ice Cream 75
Rose Water
   Rose Raspberry Ripple Ice Cream 100
Rum
   in Mojito Ice Cream 92
   in Pina Colada Ice Cream 85
   Rum & Raisin Ice Cream 86

S

Sesame Seeds
   Toasted Sesame Seed Ice Cream 64
Strawberries
   Chocolate-Covered
   Strawberries & Cream Pops 124
   in Neapolitan cake 116
   Strawberry Ice Cream 48
   Strawberry Milkshake 130

V

Vanilla
   Chamomile & Vanilla Ice Cream 96
   Extract 12
   Vanilla Ice Cream 26

W

Walnuts
   Coffee & Walnut Cake Ice Cream 82
   Maple Glazed Walnut Ice Cream 62
Wasabi
   Wasabi Ice Cream 70
Whiskey
   in Irish Cream Ice Cream 89
   Roasted Cherry & Whiskey Ice Cream 90

Wine
   White Wine Ice Cream 93

X

Xylitol
   in Sugar-free Sprinkles 152